Leading from the Front

Published in 2007 by 30° South Publishers (Pty) Ltd.
28, 9th Street, Newlands,
Johannesburg, South Africa 2092
www.30degreessouth.co.za

Copyright © John Barry, 2007

Design and origination by 30° South Publishers (Pty) Ltd.
Cover design and origination by Sven Sanders.

Printed and bound by Pinetown Printers (Pty) Ltd.

All rights reserved. No part of this publication may be reproduced, stored, manipulated in any retrieval system, or transmitted in any mechanical, electronic form or by any other means, without the prior written authority of the publishers. Any person who engages in any unauthorized activity in relation to this publication shall be liable to criminal prosecution and claims for civil and criminal damages.

ISBN 978-1-920143-11-4

Leading from the Front

John Barry

CONTENTS

Foreword by Ingrid Kast 6

Introduction by Khehla Shubane 8

Author's note 11

The early years
Chapter 1: A lonely childhood 13
Chapter 2: The value of discipline 16
Chapter 3: Starting out 22
Chapter 4: Into the hinterland 26

Shell
Chapter 5: Into the big time 32

Muller & Phipps
Chapter 6: Learning the game 40
Chapter 7: Climbing the ladder 46
Chapter 8: Something for the weekend 49
Chapter 9: The price of success 53

Friends, sport, relationships
Chapter 10: Giving life texture 56

Muller & Phipps
Chapter 11: Encounter with big brother 60
Chapter 12: Hard facts of business life 63
Chapter 13: It's not inside—it's on top 66
Chapter 14: Dancing with Pick 'n Pay 69
Chapter 15: Turning point 73

Admark
Chapter 16: A test of faith 76

Adcorp
Chapter 17: Birth of a giant 86
Chapter 18: New horizons 92
Chapter 19: Fitting it all together 95
Chapter 20: Getting burned offshore 99
Chapter 21: Leading from the front 103

Chapter 22: Listing on the JSE _____ 107
Chapter 23: It's all about the people _____ 115
Chapter 24: Argus—a failure of vision _____ 123
Chapter 25: Leading the field _____ 127
Chapter 26: A test of conscience _____ 131
Chapter 27: A brave new world _____ 136

Politics
Chapter 28: Inspired to become a true citizen _____ 140

Adcorp
Chapter 29: Seeing new opportunities _____ 145
Chapter 30: The Conversion Model _____ 148
Chapter 31: Expansion _____ 151
Chapter 32: Transformation _____ 154
Chapter 33: Building the recruitment and advertising base _____ 158

Simeka
Chapter 34: The birth of a giant and the creation of Simeka _____ 163

Adcorp
Chapter 35: Bidding for Kelly Girl _____ 170
Chapter 36: The ultimate accolade _____ 172
Chapter 37: Battles with health _____ 176

Simeka
Chapter 38: Retirement that didn't happen _____ 185
Chapter 39: A new era and a new challenge _____ 190

Life
Chapter 40: Humanizing passions _____ 197

Personal crusades
Chapter 41: Stamping out corruption _____ 202
Chapter 42: Spreading the word _____ 205

Epilogue
Chapter 43: Lessons learned _____ 208

Appendix
Adcorp awards won _____ 211

Foreword

I met John Barry during an exciting, pivotal time of my life. Adcorp had approached me to purchase DAV. John, the chairman, impressed me as a gentleman from the start. My decision was an easy one.

I have loved learning from this wise man, this all-time great and inspiring gentleman. Over the years he has mentored me and many others. John coaches you gently forward through the stories of his own experience, never prescribing your actions. He cuts through the chaff to the heart of every issue—a man who believes in simplicity. Some people just have a hunger to excel. John excels at almost everything he sets his mind to (with the possible exception of golf—the only pursuit I have ever seen bring out his Irish temper).

Throughout our friendship John has been a source of support and inspiration to me—his ethic of sheer hard work, extraordinary leadership skills, inspired and diplomatic business abilities, sharp analytical mind and genuine love of people. In conversation with John it soon becomes apparent that his heart belongs to humanity. His leadership style is based on an unerring belief in the dignity and potential of each individual. He is a very humble human being. What you see is what you get.

And yet he is tough and demanding—a disciplinarian, a no-nonsense businessman. He knows more about the acquisition of companies than anyone I have met but I have never seen him go about an acquisition with an isolated profit motive. His genius lies in identifying those companies that will be a cultural and ethical fit for his organization.

John makes everybody around him feel relaxed through his unique mix of humour (woven through his deep insightful conversation), warmth, informality and dignity. No word on John would be complete without a word on his wife Wendi. Deeply kind, loving and supportive, Wendi is John's best friend and a big part of his success. I have spent many a happy weekend with them at their bush retreat. John, although Irish by birth is a true African at heart, loves nothing more than sharing an elephant encounter with family, friends or colleagues.

Leading from the Front is written by a proven leader. It offers a magnificent cross-section of individuals and companies as well as business wisdom, anecdotes and strategy—all underpinned by John's storytelling

This is an inspiring book, full of John's conviction and insight. I am honoured to participate in it.

Ingrid Kast
CEO DAV Professional Placement; Winner of the 2006 award for the Best Company to Work for in South Africa.
Johannesburg
February 2007

Introduction

Told in the following pages is a gripping story of a man who came from nothing. He has been enriched by the cultures of people among whom he lived and at the same time limited in that he felt he lacked a commitment to any one culture. This divided feeling on this critical question is a matter about which many people have spoken and will continue to discuss—are people better off when they are rooted in a single, or multiplicity of cultures?

John describes how he finally decided to become a South African. At a time when many in his position were thinking of safer havens elsewhere he made a commitment to a land which was experiencing considerable birth pains. Inspired by Mandela he came to the conclusion that he was going to commit to the country in which he had worked and succeeded. In his particular way he has made a sterling contribution to the sustainability of the new democracy. Knowing the importance of business to a well-functioning society, he did not shy away from the controversial policy questions of the day—he threw his weight into making BEE work as it had been designed.

The book also touches on building a business from the bottom up and what a person needs to achieve this objective. Passion, energy and drive seem to be the attributes needed to build a successful business. Conspicuous on this list by its absence are high university qualifications.

Entrepreneurship, a subject taught at many business schools, remains in short supply in the world and especially in South Africa. Perhaps business studies should be structured around facilitating encounters between entrepreneurs and business students so that the former can share their experiences with the latter. Theoretical studies alone, though obviously useful, are not the answer to the dearth of entrepreneurs.

Khehla Shubane
CEO Business Map; Board member: Rand Merchant Bank, First National Bank and The Airports Authority
Johannesburg
February 2007

Author's Note

I would like to thank my good friend Ian Lints for helping me pull this book together. We spent many hours in each other's company, talking openly about events that I wanted to share. He supported and encouraged me, jogged my memory, waded through my scribbled notes and rough manuscripts and presented me with the finished article. He helped bring my story to life through his incisive writing and in doing so made an invaluable contribution

I wrote this book for my three children whom I adore. Because of circumstances, they know very little about an important phase of my life. In learning more about it I hope that we will become even closer.

I have also written this for my friends and those that I love and who love me in return. They have added immeasurably to the quality of my life.

In large part the book is dedicated to Madiba who inspired me to become a South African citizen. As each day passes I grow prouder of this wonderful land of ours.

In this great country, however humble one's background, it is possible to dream a great dream and, with a little luck on your side, you can achieve what you thought was beyond your reach.

The early years

Chapter 1

A lonely childhood

I was born on June 15 1938. I doubt whether the timing of my birth was meaningful in any greater sense, but it offers as good a starting point as any to begin this 'story'. I arrived in this world just as the second major conflict of the twentieth century was about to tear Europe apart. World War II was just around the corner, and, looking back, perhaps there was a certain resonance in this because my life, particularly my business life, has been characterized by skirmishes, conflict and battles. Inevitably some of these I've won and some I lost. Often I've come out on top, but those occasions when I have been left smarting have usually forced me to rethink, re-evaluate, re-strategize and move on, which arguably proved more valuable to me than any victory.

I was born an only child in Bushy, Hertfordshire, England. Along with thousands of other children, I was shipped out of London to the north, where it was assumed that us 'evacuees' would be in less danger from falling bombs. My mother's sister lived just outside the town of St Helens, in the northern county of Lancashire, and it was here that I stayed for the duration of the war. However, I remember very little of that time.

My mother and father were born in Ireland and were nothing if not Irish. My mother, Margaret, was from Galway and my father, John Bernard Barry, hailed from Limerick. Both were born to parents who had been teachers, my grandfather on my father's side rising through the school's ranks to become a headmaster in the area where he was born and brought up. This background of academia rubbed off on my father, who spent a large part of his life trying to master Latin, French and Greek. I also 'took' French and Latin all of my school life. I guess it was my father's education that sparked his passion for doing 'serious' crosswords. He particularly enjoyed the one in The *Times of London*; he just loved the purity of the English language and the cerebral pleasure he accrued from such puzzle-solving left a deep impression on me.

My father earned his living as an economist working for the British Government. He was primarily involved in the evaluation of major projects in various parts of the world.

For this reason, my education was effected in places as far flung as England, Egypt, Pakistan and India. Finally, as a result of my father's desire to retire to a warm climate (he had lived in many hot countries and had developed a love for sunshine) we headed to South Africa.

When I think back on my youth, I remember the world being much more formal in those days. When adult visitors came to lunch, I was not part of it. Adults ate together and I was the proverbial seen-but-not-heard child. This, I came to learn, had little to do with parental love but all to do with the etiquette of the period. On balance, I think this had its merits.

When we didn't have visitors, I would sit with my parents at lunch and my father and I would often play 'the dictionary game'. Both armed with a dictionary, over the course of the meal we would each choose ten words at random and ask the other to explain their meanings. Invariably I was hugely frustrated at having to read out words—particularly those that were French, Latin or Greek derivatives that I could barely pronounce. I had to spell them, and to my huge frustration my father always knew every one—or at least that's how it seemed back then.

However, it was a game that was fun and one I always looked forward to. As a result I developed an interest in the English language that has stayed with me ever since. Later in life I used a similar technique with my own three children. We would play games where we would have sheets of paper, with letters of the alphabet across the top and headings down the side of countries, capitals, prime ministers and major rivers. We would each choose a heading of a subject we enjoyed and I'd pick the more difficult ones, such as the capital cities category. In the same way my father tried with me, the design was to broaden their knowledge.

While we lived in Egypt, Pakistan and India I didn't particularly relish the school holidays. Going home at the end of the boarding school year was a lonely experience as there wasn't a single person that I knew from school living anywhere near me. I was an only child and there was simply nobody for me to talk to or play with, although now and again I would play tennis with my father.

From India we went back to England, our last stop before South Africa. By some odd symmetrical quirk, I went to grammar school in St Helen's, the very same town I had been shipped off to during the war.

But my schooling proved a great embarrassment. I had two cousins, who were a number of years older than me. Both were very intelligent and high achievers and had been head boys at the grammar school. They went on to become headmasters and one subsequently became a professor at Manchester University. It was assumed that, as a member of the family, I would follow in their footsteps. However, in my first year I came 42nd out of a class of 43, even though I was really trying. I simply could not fathom maths and algebra in particular was beyond me. I couldn't get the grasp of geometry and I really disliked poetry. I had neither a love nor feeling for history, and was totally hopeless at art. The only thing I was any good at was geography, an interest undoubtedly stoked by all my travelling.

Because of all of the travelling that we did—and because we were always fairly closeted in whatever country we lived—we did not move in what might be described as the broader social world. Despite this, my mother was very much a woman of her era as well as her background. She was always a most loving and kind mother and obviously a wonderful wife and partner to my father. Tragically, she suffered very badly from rheumatoid arthritis, which in the end crippled her to the point where she could barely walk. She suffered a great deal in silence and my memory of her suffering is accompanied by an image of my father permanently at her side. He was always there for her and with her. He was a very kindly man, and in the proper sense of the word he truly was a gentle man as well as a gentleman. Thank God she lived long enough to see her two grandchildren.

Chapter 2

The value of discipline

As mentioned, my father was a gentleman to the core. Even in his autumn years and growing somewhat frail he always stood up whenever a lady entered the room and would remain standing until everyone was seated. This small gesture left an indelible impression on me and I often think that his Victorian values belonged to a bygone age.

I never heard him raise his voice or resort to abusive language even when he was provoked. I have an abiding memory of him on an occasion when he was admonishing one of our household staff. I can't recall why he was so outraged but he managed to retain his dignified demeanour.

He took me aside after the incident and said firmly, "John, always remember that the use of well-chosen words allows you to make your point far more powerfully. Don't ever be tempted to resort to foul language because if you do, you will only lower yourself in the eyes of others. It will show the world that you can't express yourself without using vulgarities."

We hadn't been in South Africa very long, I was about fifteen at the time. I was returning from the tennis club with a young girl at my side.

My father happened to be walking on the opposite side of the road and I noticed him eyeing me intently. As I entered the house minutes later, he tackled me. "Have you any idea what you did today?"

I was taken aback and I stammered out some sort of lame reply imagining that I had not completed a job that I was supposed to do.

He said in a stern tone, "You allowed that girl by your side to walk on the outside of you on the pavement!"

That was probably the last time I committed that particular gaffe. He instilled in me the importance of good manners and how enormously important they are in life.

At every opportunity my father impressed upon me that every person however humble, mighty, cultured or ignorant was an equal and was entitled to dignity. He insisted that everybody should always be treated with humanity and respect. Apart from teaching me the value of self-discipline it was one of the most important lessons I learned from him. Throughout my life I have endeavoured to pass these values on to my children.

When my father accepted a position in India it meant that the family had to pack up and take the long sea voyage to Calcutta. As soon as we arrived I was packed off to St Joseph's College, a boarding school that was tucked away in the foothills of the Himalayas a few kilometres outside Darjeeling.

I took to boarding school life like a duck to water. Living under a strict disciplinary regime and being separated from one's parents for months on end didn't agree with everyone but I absolutely loved it. The education that I received at St Josephs was better by a long chalk than at any other school in any of the other countries where we'd lived. The Jesuit priests continually strove to attain high scholastic standards and the three and a half years that I spent at St Josephs had a major influence in shaping my early years.

At the beginning of each school year the arduous journey from Calcutta to Darjeeling began with a one-hour flight to a small airport in the foothills of the Himalayas. I would transfer to Siliguri station by rickshaw where I met the other boys and then we would pile into the train for the eight-hour train journey into the mountains on a narrow-gauge line. The track slowly winds up through the tea plantations and I always looked forward to the trip. I couldn't help marvelling at how ingenious the engineers had been to build the line. It made four complete loops and there were five switchbacks as it chugged slowly up through the bazaars of Ghoom and Darjeeling.

When we finally arrived at Darjeeling station, we were met by one of the Jesuit priests who escorted us to the school. St Joseph's is situated about three kilometres out of town and it could have been transplanted from somewhere in the English shires. The first time we drove through the gates of St Josephs it reminded me of the books I'd read about Billy Bunter at Greyfriars. The imposing grey stone buildings, quadrangle and sports fields perched high up on a ridge were totally incongruous after the chaos and oppressive heat of Calcutta.

Darjeeling originally became popular as a cool summer refuge for the British troops in the mid-1800s. On a clear day one could gaze across to the snowy peaks of Kanchenjunga. Far below in the valley you could see the swollen rivers and the seemingly endless sea of tea bushes covering the terraced hillsides.

Because of soaring summer temperatures and monsoon rains in most of India, the school year started at the end of January and lasted until mid-November and boarders weren't allowed home in between. Being away from home for nearly ten months was probably unique to schools in Northern India.

There was a short holiday break in the middle of the school year in June and July during which parents were allowed to take boarders out of school for a week. If, however, we got written permission from our parents we were allowed to spend the holidays with a friend. My close friend was the son of a minor maharajah and although I later discovered that he didn't exactly live in a palace, I recall that the house was very opulent and that there were servants lurking around every corner. One day we embarked on a tiger hunt and I sat high up on the back of an elephant while the beaters crashed about in the undergrowth. Needless to say we never saw a tiger that day but it certainly provided me with bragging rights when I returned to school.

There were nearly six hundred boarders from all over the East—China, Indonesia, Korea, as well as many, of course, from India and St Josephs achieved prominence because many wealthy Indian maharajahs insisted on sending their sons there to prepare them for Oxford or Cambridge. However, many boys were like me; the sons of expatriates working in various places on the Indian sub-continent and here we received an education that replicated the English public school system.

We were encouraged to strive for scholastic excellence but great emphasis was also placed on rounding out our education with extra-curricular activities. Every conceivable interest was catered for and music teachers were keen to conscript any boy showing the slightest inclination to join piano, violin or brass instrument classes. I am blessed with fairly long fingers and my mother's parting words when I kissed her goodbye were, "Now John, please don't forget to enrol for piano lessons."

So, based purely on being blessed with longer than average fingers I duly enrolled for piano lessons. After a couple of weeks my teacher concluded that I was not only tone deaf, but that I was incapable of mastering 'Chopsticks', the starting point for any budding concert pianist. Though I protested that my long fingers would eventually navigate around the keyboard the teacher advised me to call it a day. Driven on by my mother's belief that I possessed a latent musical talent, I moved to the violin class. Not only did the violin teacher have even less patience with my efforts than my piano teacher but she was considerably more forthright.

After less than a week she bluntly told me, "John you have absolutely no ear for music and you are just wasting everyone's time."

Sadly for my mother, on a scale from one to ten I scored zero in the world of music. The realization that I had no aptitude for music was a bitter pill to swallow. I mulled over alternative avenues that might bring me more success and eventually my logic dictated that sporting activity was where I could best make my mark. Bearing in mind that I was small for my age it probably came as a surprise to my school chums when I announced that I would take up boxing. I came to this decision without any real thought that I might be totally unsuited to the rough and tumble of the ring and it certainly never crossed my mind that I might actually sustain a bloody nose or worse.

On my first visit to the gymnasium I was given a rudimentary set of instructions about self-defence and then the gloves were strapped on and I was hustled into the ring. I raised my gloves and danced on my feet, but an immediate feeling of trepidation overtook me. This lack of confidence was borne from the fact that fighting was not something that came naturally as I'd never had a real skirmish in my young life and I had never experienced a blow to the nose. I shuffled toward my opponent and we sized each other up. I moved in cautiously. After I'd thrown a couple of wild swings, none of which connected, my adversary began hitting me at will. I tried desperately to respond but every time he landed a blow my natural instinct was to close my eyes. Bruised and shaken, the fight was called to a halt, and my record on my first outing read: fights one, losses one. After two more crushing defeats, during which I failed to land a single adequate blow, my instructor led me aside and gently suggested that I looked elsewhere for an extra-curricular activity more suited to my talents.

St Joseph's College placed great emphasis on strict discipline and this was reinforced at every turn. Each evening after supper the boys would file silently into the Great Hall for two hours of private study. We sat at our desks working on our assignments under the eagle eye of a priest. One of our weekly study time tasks was to compose a letter to our parents. To ensure that we didn't shirk the exercise, we had to show our completed note to the supervising priest who sat perched on a raised podium.

He would scrutinize the content of our letter and place it into an envelope. He also enclosed our weekly 'scorecard' with the letter and mailed it to our parents. This scorecard held the key to our fate when it came to claiming our privileges. Each week every pupil was marked in six categories ranging from behaviour in the classroom to the manner in which we conducted ourselves in the dormitory, during study and in the dining room. A score of twenty was the ultimate, but needless to say I never achieved this exulted mark. If you managed to get twenty you were awarded a gold card, nineteen down to sixteen got you a blue card and so on. We all tried to escape a score of below twelve because that earned you four cuts with a rattan cane and you were denied the pleasure of a monthly trip into Darjeeling. If anybody ever received three grey cards for a score of less than ten it resulted in automatic expulsion.

Privileges were something to be cherished, and if you couldn't walk down to town it was a devastating blow, because we all looked forward to visiting Glenary's teashop to spend our pocket money on cakes and to stock up with sweets. We had to wear our uniform for these outings and should we encounter one of the tea planters or his memsahib in the village we had to doff our caps as a mark of respect. A poor scorecard also meant that you were automatically excluded from one of the regular weekend camping trips into the foothills of Darjeeling. Actually we rarely ventured beyond one of the many tea plantations in the area during these forays, but the idea of sleeping out in the open seemed rather exciting at the time. After all, we could imagine the tigers lurking in the night.

During one particular holiday, when I arrived home my mother presented me with a puppy on a leash and I thought that I would faint from excitement. At the time we were living in a fairly modest but comfortable house in a compound outside Calcutta on the banks of the Hooghly River. Many of the British expatriates stayed there and in common with most of them we had a bevy of servants to cater to our every need. I had little contact with any of them but I quickly learned that they had their own hierarchy. There was the *jamadar* who came from the lowest caste and his sole task was to clean the windows and floors. The head of the household was the butler and all the other servants reported to him. The butler ran the house with clockwork precision and he attended to all my father's personal needs. I recall how, when my father returned from work, the butler would remove his shoes for him, run his bath and place a cold beer on a side table.

I think that there is often a misconception that people who have achieved financial success simply had one great idea and then, as if by magic, it made them a fortune. Maybe there are exceptions, but I wasn't smart enough to do it that way. In my case any success that I enjoyed resulted from plain hard work. In the early days at Admark I rarely put in less than ten to twelve hours a day and I often spent my weekends working. Certainly if I learned anything at St Josephs it was discipline. As I developed I realized just how important the lessons my father taught me were and how much they shaped my business thinking. On reflection, I believe that self discipline is as vital to the success of every businessman as is his determination to achieve success by sheer hard work.

In my wildest stretch of imagination I cannot claim to have reached any academic heights at St Josephs. Even when I came to South Africa I didn't set the world alight but my marks began to improve when I began to take subjects like chemistry and physics. I never excelled at any particular subject because in spite of working reasonably hard my mind was usually distracted by my interest in sport.

My athletic prowess was probably inherited from my father who excelled on the football field. Tennis was my first love and I derived great personal satisfaction from winning a few minor tournaments. I have few treasured mementoes, but shortly before he died my father gave me a gold medal shaped as a Gallic cross. It was awarded to him in 1924 when he was capped by Ireland at soccer and it is inscribed with his name 'JB Barry', I cherish this beautiful memento so dearly that I had replicas struck for each of my children. There is never a time when I don't wear mine and it's now eighty years old.

Chapter 3

Starting out

I was fifteen when we arrived in South Africa. It was my father's intention to settle down, but within two years he was on the move again. He couldn't say no when he was offered the chance to manage another huge project in Pakistan. We all understood that it was a tempting offer and one that he couldn't turn down, but I couldn't hide my disappointment.

I had adjusted well to life in Durban and the thought of moving yet again filled me with dread. My parents tried hard to persuade me and they both made desperate pleas for me to go with them to Pakistan. In spite of my mothers strongest arguments, I finally won the day and I was allowed to stay.

When it was time for them to leave I had mixed feelings. It struck me that at approaching seventeen I would be alone, cast adrift to fend for myself. A wave of emptiness swept over me. One of the reasons I fought so hard to remain in Durban was that I realized I didn't have an anchor. I had no foundations, no lifelong friends, no roots and more importantly no loyalties.

I was an avid sports fan but I didn't feel passionate about any national team. Whenever I watched an international soccer or cricket match I felt more like an outsider looking on. I felt like a neutral and I envied the fervour and depth of feeling that seemed to come so naturally to my South African friends. I wished more than anything else that I could be like that.

This identity crisis was bought to a head the day I decided to stay in South Africa. It was something of a watershed and from that moment I was determined to cultivate a sense of national pride.

My schooling was bought to an abrupt halt as soon as I completed standard eight (now grade ten). I didn't have a clue how I would support myself or what I wanted to do with my life. I was adrift and rudderless. And so, very much alone and without even some distant aunt to call on I was forced into manhood.

I managed to get a job at Barclays Bank in Durban. I felt very proud of myself and on my first day I decided that if this was the way people earned a crust, life would be pretty easy. I couldn't believe my luck; all I had to do every day was accompany a colleague on the drive to our branch office in Amanzimtoti. We would then bundle huge sums of cash into a suitcase and head back to Durban. Looking back it seems amazing how casual we were about the whole procedure but it was of course long before bank robberies or cash-in-transit heists were commonplace. Nowadays armed guards ride shotgun but in our case the teller accompanying me carried a gun in a holster more for show; he was never actually expected to use it. Nevertheless, my vivid imagination ran riot and I gave rein to my cops and robbers fantasies. It was very exciting to think that one day I might be involved in a major shootout. I spent three years in the bank and ended up laboriously writing up ledgers in Musgrave Road where there wasn't the remotest chance of raising my pulse rate. I was bored to death and I knew that a long and distinguished career in banking was not going to be for me.

About this time I discovered that sport was not the only thing to occupy the minds of hot-blooded young men. Girls were really a rather attractive proposition. The problem facing me was how I could possibly manage to snare one. The drawback was that I certainly didn't appear to possess any of the natural attributes that were apparently needed. When I left school I was somewhat vertically challenged and although I did sprout to average height by the time I was twenty-two my cause wasn't assisted by a face covered in freckles. If that wasn't bad enough I had a shock of bright red hair that wouldn't lie down unless I plastered it with a bottle of Brylcreem.

Shortly after my parents left South Africa my father began remitting a monthly sum of money to Durban and after about two years a substantial balance had built up in his savings account. When I received a letter from him I was left in no doubt what I had to do.

"John, I know that it is just a waste of time having my funds lying in the bank earning a paltry amount of interest. I want you to withdraw it all and do something with it."

I was excited by the thought and was proud that my father had shown so much trust in my judgement. I was elated to think that he considered me responsible enough to grow his nest egg. At eighteen, like most men of my age, I was supremely confident that even with my very limited commercial knowledge I'd be successful.

I cast around for a suitable enterprise that I could buy with my relatively limited funds and within weeks I had invested my father's savings in a tiny tearoom near the Durban beachfront. I was exhilarated to be in business for myself and I didn't mind in the least that the pokey premises were barely fifty square metres.

Even today I am not at my best in the early morning but in those days it was a monumental effort to struggle down to the tearoom at the crack of dawn. And even my three years at St Josephs when I had to get up at six and wash in cold water wasn't adequate preparation!

I'd arrive bleary eyed at around six thirty and at that unearthly hour there was nobody else in the streets other than a couple of night watchmen who were preparing to go off duty. Crates of fresh milk, bread and pastries in boxes that had been delivered hours before were already stacked on the pavement outside the shop. It never entered my head that anyone could have helped themselves to an early breakfast as things like that just didn't happen in those days. I'd spend half an hour unpacking the goods onto the shelves and then throw the doors open for business. I was still working at the bank so I hired an assistant to help out and she used to arrive just in time for me to rush off to my daytime job. After spending the whole day writing up ledgers at the bank I'd return to the shop to relieve my assistant and I'd put in a three-hour stint behind the counter. I'd then close up shop, cash up and by that time I was so exhausted that all I wanted to do was go home and crash out. Because I tried to cut down on expenses in order to make a small profit, my assistant didn't work on weekends. Instead, I'd run the place on Saturdays and Sundays. Unfortunately, this meant that I couldn't apply myself to the pressing problem of how to attract the opposite sex!

I began to think more and more about how I could find some redeeming feature that would make me irresistible to young ladies, considering my total lack of physical presence. I mulled over several possibilities of marketing myself and eventually concluded that it would impress the girls if I expanded my mind. I called in to Durban Technical College and almost on a whim I signed on for a CIS (now ICSA) course of evening lectures. This new commitment meant locking up the shop just before eight and rushing to college for the start of lectures. It was a nightmarish period during which I was doing fifteen-hour days. This went on for almost two years until my father arrived back in South Africa.

My father was somewhat taken aback by my choice of investment as I'm sure that it never entered his head that I would chose to sink his funds in a tearoom. However, when he found out that his original capital had grown considerably, he was very happy with me. He eventually sold the business for a healthy profit and the proceeds were enough for him to buy a small residential hotel on the Berea. This venture provided him with a regular income well into his retirement.

Chapter 4

Into the hinterland

As a fairly lowly employee at the bank I could only fantasize about owning a car. Most months there was virtually nothing left over from my salary cheque after I'd paid my living expenses. However, by scrimping and saving I managed to scrape together enough cash to buy a second-hand Vespa scooter and this became my pride and joy.

With the brashness typical of youth, I boasted to my colleagues at the bank that I could go anywhere on the scooter. One day one of the tellers challenged me and my bravado was momentarily shaken.

"John, you are very cocky about where you can go on that machine, but I bet you ten quid that you'd never make it to Lourenço Marques (now Maputo) and back over the Easter weekend."

I suppose that what I lacked in grey matter, I made up for in confidence. In short, I was fearless, foolhardy and not too bright. I had been backed into a corner but I came out fighting.

"Don't worry, I'll be there and back with time to spare and your tenner will help pay for the petrol."

I had absolutely no idea about the state of the road to the Mozambican border or even exactly where or how far it was and, as the big day approached, I began to doubt the wisdom of my bet.

I persuaded Richard Dumbrill, a close friend, to join me on this hair-raising trip. Richard incidentally later went on to play cricket for Natal and South Africa but at the time he was as naïve as I was. By mid-afternoon on the Thursday before Easter the two of us set off. Richard was perched on the pillion while I sat rather awkwardly with a tiny case containing our clothes balanced between my legs on the running board. Not only did this put us in mortal danger, but after an hour's riding I was stiff and saddle sore. The suitcase made it virtually impossible for me to use the foot brake and I feared that if I was forced into an emergency stop we'd be in deep trouble.

We pressed on north to Stanger and just as we were congratulating ourselves on making such good progress I became distracted. As we entered the outskirts of the town I blithely sailed through a red traffic light. I also failed to notice until the very last moment that a police van had stopped in front of us. In a blind panic I tried to hit the foot brake but I got my foot stuck behind the suitcase and ended up crashing into the rear end of the police van. Thankfully the policeman was more worried about what damage I'd done to his van. After satisfying himself that his vehicle was unscathed, he nonchalantly waved me on. It was a narrow squeak and we breathed a sigh of relief but as a result of the collision we sustained a smashed headlight. We agreed then that driving after dark was no longer a safe option.

I soon regained my composure and we continued north in high spirits. Suddenly the tarmac ran out and we hit a rutted dirt road. Darkness began to close in but, throwing caution to the wind and ignoring our own advice, we forged on without lights. The road seemed to go on endlessly but we refused to admit defeat, so we plunged into the night until around midnight when we pulled into Gollel (now Golela), the southern border town between South Africa and Mozambique.

I'd never embarked on an expedition remotely like this trip to Mozambique and neither of us had a clue that international border posts could conceivably close at night. The barriers were pulled down and the area around the frontier was absolutely deserted. All we could see were a couple of isolated buildings in the distance. We hunted around and eventually managed to find a small shop with a wraparound veranda, where we huddled in a corner and spent a cold and very uncomfortable night.

When the border officials pitched up for duty at six o'clock they were rather surprised to be confronted by two dishevelled and highly agitated young men. They stamped our passports, perfunctorily checked the scooter and waved us on our way. We leapt on the scooter, hit the throttle and drove like crazy until, totally exhausted, we reached Lourenço Marques on Good Friday afternoon.

Before we set out from Durban the notion of prebooking our accommodation never entered our heads and not surprisingly, as it was a long weekend, everywhere we tried was choc-a-bloc. We were on the verge of giving up when we pulled up outside a nondescript little guesthouse in a side street. I sent Richard inside to check it out while I sat astride the scooter and resigned myself to yet another disappointment. He came back with a wry smile on his face that I assumed meant we'd be sleeping on the beach.

"We're in luck but don't expect too much. Actually the owner said that the place was full but he took pity on me and said that he'd squeeze us in."

"What's the catch, I suppose there's not even a shower in the room?"

"Not exactly. In fact we'll be sleeping in the corridor," said Richard rather sheepishly. We couldn't wait to unpack our gear and go exploring. To be honest we hoped that with a slice of luck we'd be able to hook up with a couple of girls and check out the nightlife with them. With horror I discovered that I'd forgotten to pack my trousers! Richard too, hardly looked sartorial in his crumpled suit so all in all we didn't hold out high hopes of creating a favourable impression.

Just about the only tip we'd picked up before setting out from Durban came from our local Portuguese vegetable shop owner. When we told him that we were heading up to Mozambique his eyes glazed over and with a nod and a wink he said, "Whatever you do, don't miss the Penguin nightclub."

Not having too much experience with seedy clubs we assumed that if we arrived slightly early we'd have a better choice of tables and girls. We were ushered into a dimly lit and distinctly shabby room. The host seated us, took our drinks order and drifted off. We swiftly ascertained that we were the only patrons in the club and that we'd probably have to wait for another three hours or so before things livened up. When our eyes became accustomed to the light we noticed that there was a line of chairs against the wall on which were seated a bevy of highly painted ladies. The youngest was probably around fourteen and the oldest could easily have been our grandmother. We could take our pick from a dusky and seductive schoolgirl to a pouting ebony temptress of a hundred and twenty kilograms!

In our naïvety we hadn't realized that patrons were expected to select a lady of their choice and invite them to join them at their table.

Seconds after the waiter arrived with our soft drinks two heavyweight hostesses with rouged lips and a liberal application of make-up on their cheeks pulled up their chairs and indicated that they too were thirsty. They motioned to the waiter and asked him to bring a bottle of Moët & Chandon champagne. This triggered off alarm bells and I realized that we were in way above our heads.

"No ! We don't want champagne just bring the bill for our Cokes."

I turned to Richard and whispered urgently, "Let's get out of this place before we get fleeced."

The hostesses were not deflected that easily and they summoned the bouncer over to our table. As he towered above us he appeared to be the size of a Durban bus. I was petrified, not only scared out of my wits but worried what effect this little escapade would have on our severely limited financial resources. After feigning ignorance of the club's etiquette I emptied all the cash in our wallets onto the table as evidence that we couldn't afford another round of drinks even if we wanted to. The bouncer grabbed us by the scruff of our necks and bundled us unceremoniously onto the pavement outside.

We returned to our guesthouse around midnight and bedded down but sleep eluded us. Most of the guests seemed to have been drinking beer all evening and had bursting bladders. The route to the communal bathrooms involved the guests stepping clumsily over our recumbent bodies and so the corridor was more like a pedestrian mall than a bedroom.

On Saturday we packed our suitcase and headed toward Johannesburg but the atrocious road conditions made for slow going and we only made it as far as Belfast in the Eastern Transvaal (now Mpumalanga) by nightfall. The hotel that we checked into had traffic thundering past within metres of our room, but it was sheer luxury to be sleeping in a bed for the night.

For all my boasting about the performance of the Vespa I had to admit that I was finding it impossible to average more than sixty-five kilometres an hour. I calculated that to have any hope of winning the bet and reaching Durban by Monday we'd have to leave Belfast at four in the morning. So riding all day and through the night without either headlights or brakes we staggered into Durban at two in the morning the following day. We'd been on the road for about twenty-two hours. My legs were numb and my body cried out from acute muscle cramps and my wrists were desperately sore from being locked to the throttle.

The next morning I sauntered into work and although the act of walking was painful I tried to appear rather nonchalant. A group of expectant colleagues gathered around, curious to see how we had fared. I turned to the guy I'd struck the bet with and said, "It was dead easy. Next Easter we'll make it to Salisbury and back. You owe me ten quid."

The Vespa gave sterling service for many years afterward although its condition gradually deteriorated until it finally gave up the ghost when the throttle cable snapped. Being penniless, I couldn't afford to fix it so I disconnected the foot brake and connected the throttle cable to the foot brake.

I managed to get along without any major incident but when my great friend Mick Feuilherade asked to borrow the Vespa I had a sinking feeling. Mick and I were inseparable and we did absolutely everything together. Mick was handsome and smooth in an Errol Flynn kind of way and girls flocked to him like bees around a honey pot. I enjoyed basking in his reflected glory because not only was he fun to be with, but I always held out hope that if any of the girls were rebuffed by him that I could snare them on the rebound. In practice this rarely happened, but nonetheless we did our fair share of partying and hell-raising together.

When I handed over the scooter I carefully explained to him that he'd have to be pretty alert in an emergency.

His response was less than reassuring, "Don't worry John, I'll be okay"

A few days later he limped into my flat and his explanation was as predictable as day follows night, "Everything was fine until a dog ran out in front of me. I hit the brake and I completely forgot what I should do and accelerated through a hedge!"

Mick has since moved to Cape Town and I have settled in Johannesburg and gradually as the years passed we drifted apart but I will always hold fond memories of our many escapades.

Shell

Chapter 5

Into the big time

For a while I couldn't work out why I was having such a spectacular lack of success with girls. Then it dawned on me—my low self-esteem stemmed from my lack of inches, my rash of freckles and my flame-red hair. Yes, they were partly to blame, but I saw these as only minor obstacles. All that was needed to turn things around was a set of wheels.

There was one slight snag. The chance of owning a car was a pipe dream. On my less than generous bank salary I simply had no hope of scraping enough cash together. One day I was beavering away at a bank ledger when I began daydreaming about cruising through Durban in a sports car with a nubile young blonde beside me. The answer to my dilemma came to me in a blinding flash. The solution was so simple that I wondered why I hadn't thought of it before. I'd get a job as a salesman!

People were always commenting on my gift of the gab and I seemed to get on very well with most people. That was it; I had all the skills needed to become a professional salesman. I'd apply for a job, get a company car and bingo!—I'd be in business.

I answered an advertisement for a sales job with Shell and when the inevitable question arose about why I wanted the job, I glibly answered that I had always wanted to be a salesman and that I had all the qualities needed. If only the personnel manager had been able to read my mind my answer would have been, "Sir, if you give me the job the girls will be falling all over me."

To my amazement, Shell offered me a position, but unfortunately not as a salesman. My hopes were dashed on the car front when I was posted to the accounts department. My immediate objective was thwarted but because of Shell's progressive policy on staff development, I received a magnificent all-round training including a comprehensive grounding in sales and marketing.

It took me another four years to rise to the exulted position of sales representative. I was in seventh heaven when I was given a company car. The only drawback was that I was assigned to Kokstad and I soon found out that the only girls in that area were under the age of seventeen. The first thing any of them did when they passed matric was leave town for good!

After a few months, I was invited to participate in a sales and marketing course at the company training headquarters in Muizenberg. I looked forward to the Dale Carnegie public speaking part, as I rather fancied myself as a polished and assured orator. I thought that it would be the perfect opportunity to impress the bosses when I delivered my speech to the other forty or so participants.

Everyone was asked to address the assembled delegates with a three-minute speech and I cruised through it. I thought that I'd been quite smooth and assured with my confidence running high for what was to come. Unlike many of the others, I wasn't unduly worried by the thought of speaking for three minutes on a mystery subject that would only be disclosed to me as I was called to the podium.

As we got further into the course, the impromptu speeches became longer and the director sought to identify and probe our irritating mannerisms and halting or mumbled speech. If you fiddled with your tie or jangled the keys in your pocket, he encouraged the audience to give you a hard time and for anyone the least bit nervous it was very intimidating.

The more nervous participants would try to learn their prepared speeches off by heart. They wanted to avoid being caught on the hop but, to counteract it, the director introduced a particularly off-putting distraction. As you got out of your stride, everyone would begin clicking their fingers in unison. It was very funny to listen to people completely lose track of whatever subject they were trying to get across to the audience. Most would go a complete blank and have to begin again while others were totally destroyed and abandoned the podium in embarrassment.

Unknown to the delegates, the chief executive Len Abrahamse and two other senior executives at Shell joined us for dinner on the final night. Len later moved through the ranks of Shell International and went on to carve out a very distinguished career in the financial world. During dinner, the course director revealed that he had selected the three most accomplished speakers to deliver unprepared speeches to the dinner guests and I was delighted to hear that I was one of those chosen.

My name was drawn out of a hat first and I was called forward to deliver a seven-minute, unprepared speech. I was supremely confident until I unfolded the slip of paper that was passed to me. The subject stopped me in my tracks. I swallowed hard and desperately tried to gather my thoughts. My hands were shaking as I confronted the audience and my throat began to constrict. I forced myself to relax and began.

"Ladies, gentlemen and distinguished guests, tonight I would like to speak to you about the love life of the African camel!"

The idea of attempting to bamboozle us with difficult or obscure subjects was designed to equip us to think on our feet. The course helped delegates to confront difficult situations and it enabled them to converse on subjects that were often alien to them. This concept didn't help me much as I haltingly worked my way through the first few seconds of my speech. Something that stuck in my mind from the lessons was that if you flounder, you can often get out of a tight corner by being funny. Humour, however, can be a dangerous twin-edged sword and unless you are in tune with your audience it can fall very flat.

I decided to go out on a limb and I began to relax a little.

"You probably know from your visits to the zoo that there are two types of camel. There is the Dromedary and the Bacterian but don't ask me which is which."

I paused to gauge the reaction and I was happy to hear a titter ripple through the audience.

"When I was a boy I went to school in Egypt and everyday I used to pass an old man who owned two camels. Each camel had its humps covered with a strange garment and at the end of the day, the old man used to carry water in them. Years later I found out that these covers were the prototype for today's bras."

Again I halted, but this time the audience's reaction was more muted. Stunned would perhaps a better word. It just wasn't funny and I learned a valuable lesson—avoid the use of humour like the plague unless you can be sure to carry it off. The final minutes of my speech turned into a rambling and incoherent babble and needless to say I finished in a distant third place.

I gained invaluable experience in my early days as a salesman and I was happy enough when I was asked to deputize for an employee who'd been fired. I was sent to Estcourt for three weeks to manage the depot but what was supposed to be a short sojourn turned out to be an eighteen-month stay.

As soon as we closed up at midday on Saturdays I used to jump into my Morris Minor and head for Durban. I'd meet my friend Mick and we'd watch sport and party into the early hours. Completely drained I would reluctantly head back to Estcourt in time to start work on Monday morning. My time in Estcourt did little to satisfy my drive to meet girls because, just like Kokstad, after matric they all vanished into thin air! It really did appear that I was destined to be in the wrong place at the wrong time!

In 1960 I was finally offered a position at Shell's regional office in Durban and I grabbed the chance with both hands. I was made area manager for the Gas Division and although it was the smallest division in the company I really felt that I was beginning to go places. I felt proud when the CEO appointed me because at just twenty-four I became the youngest divisional manager in the South African company's history.

Shortly afterward I had my first brush with death.

On many weekends I got together with a bunch of friends and we would drive up to the Cathedral Peak Hotel in the Drakensberg. In those days it was a low-key and slightly downbeat place and a million miles from today's luxury establishment. We were such regular visitors that it was almost like going home for the weekend and what the place lacked in finesse was more than made up for by its party atmosphere.

One Saturday morning we were on our way to the Drakensberg when,

Leading from the Front

just outside Durban, not far from Hillcrest I was involved in a head-on smash. I was behind the wheel and I took the full brunt of the impact. I was rushed to Grey's Hospital in Pietermaritzburg. My legs were numb and all I could think of was that I'd spend the rest of my life in a wheelchair.

I suppose I could say that I was fortunate to sustain nothing more than a dislocated spine. Lucky is not a word that I use lightly because my friend who was sitting behind me was killed instantly, while my other two friends walked away from the accident totally unscathed.

The result of this horrific accident was that I was forced to wear a plaster cast from my neck to my hips for over six months. It was inconvenient and most uncomfortable because I had to wear it during the height of summer. The intense heat and humidity caused the perspiration to trickle down into the cast and the constant itch drove me insane.

It didn't help that I wasn't allowed to get the plaster cast wet so I had to manoeuvre myself on to the edge of the bath whenever I needed to wash. After a few weeks I became extremely self conscious about the unpleasant smell of stale perspiration that emanated from the cast and I worried that my friends had just been too polite to tell me. I must have got through several dozen cans of baby powder to help mask the odour and eventually I began to smell more like a baby than a polecat. I never went anywhere without arming myself with a long knitting needle to scratch the itchy spots and a can of baby powder.

Every time that I went for my monthly examination Dr Mungo Thompson, the surgeon who put me in the cast, constantly impressed on me the importance of keeping fit. He warned me that I shouldn't allow my muscles to waste away.

Playing rugby or offering my services to the local cricket club as a fast bowler were clearly not the answer. Nevertheless I was naturally pretty active and I suggested to my friends that if they went easy on me I could manage a gentle game of squash. Mick was very patient during our games at the Caister Hotel court and he never made me feel awkward because I couldn't manage to run or bend. I just used to stand around in the centre of the court while he lobbed the ball gently back and forth to me.

This form of gentle exercise soon became boring and I persuaded my friends that I could probably handle a round of golf. Mick was dubious, "You'll never be able to swing a club in that state."

We pitched up at Isipingo Golf Club. I couldn't have been more nervous if I was playing in the US Open because the first tee was situated in full view of several members who were sitting in the clubhouse.

Mick whispered, "John, let's get on with it. Don't worry about the rules; just pick the bloody ball up and walk the first two holes. Then you can play on without being put under pressure."

I reacted stubbornly because I wanted to play properly or not at all. I pulled out my driver and addressed the ball. My friends held their breath. I became acutely aware of the plaster cast resting on my hips. It was shaped to fit just under my armpits and I wore it under my shirt like a corset. To anyone watching I probably appeared to be like a walking tailor's dummy. My friends were agitated because I was moving so slowly. The foursome waiting to tee off behind us was becoming impatient.

Minutes passed and everyone watching fell silent and began to stare intently. The club members were probably murmuring about how disgraceful it was for me to attempt to play while I was inebriated. When I squatted stiffly beside the tee and stood up and prepared to address the ball, the onlookers began to laugh openly. I flexed my arms and without as much as a practice swing I launched into my first shot.

The whoosh of air told me that I had missed by a mile but to add insult to injury the momentum of my swing and the weight of my plaster cast was enough to send me sprawling flat on my face. Mick helped me to my feet and said urgently, "Everybody thinks you're drunk so just pick the ball up. We'll never be allowed back here if we don't get moving."

I gritted my teeth and barked back at him, "No chance. I don't care if I'm here till midnight, I'm going to hit this ball down the fairway and everyone else must just wait."

I had clearly lost all sense of proportion and I was oblivious to the embarrassment I was inflicting on my friends.

I put my wood back in my bag and took out an iron and I thought that I'd just try to hit the ball forty metres. I steadied myself and told myself to swing easily. Yet again in spite of taking a short back swing there was the swishing sound of club on fresh air.

The whole episode was descending into farce and my friends were urging me to give up. Once again Mick pleaded with me to pick up the ball and move on. "Mick, leave me alone. You can go if you want, but I am sure that this time I can do better. Even if it only goes twenty metres I'm going to hit this ball."

At the third attempt I took an incredibly gentle swing and adrenaline surged through me as I felt the ball fly off the iron. I stepped back and as I did so Mick said, "That's all we need. You just sliced the ball through the clubhouse window."

I later went cap in hand to explain to the club secretary what had happened but I refused to use my injury as an excuse. Somebody had probably told him how a drunken young fool had made a spectacle of himself, but he kept a stiff upper lip and accepted my apology with good grace.

I didn't finish the round. I hit a few shots and stayed out of trouble. The cast chafed my hips and underarms and I had to admit that golf was still a bridge too far for a man with a dislocated back.

Besides that though, life was good. I was working long hours and loving every moment, and I had developed a relationship with Sue, who also worked at Shell. I proposed within months of meeting her and she agreed to marry me. It was at this point that, for the first time in my life, the issue of money or more specifically the lack of it, raised its ugly head.

I was managing a team of salesmen but when I discovered that every single one of them was earning more than me, I became angry. When I confronted my boss to ask why, his explanation did nothing to placate me.

"You have to understand, John, that you are still only twenty-four. Most of the guys that work for you are over forty and they've been with the company for donkey's years. They started at the bottom on a low basic salary but over time with annual increases it stands to reason that they should be earning more than you."

I mulled over his reply and tried to control my emotions.

"But that's rubbish. People should be paid according to what they do and not how old they are! I am not happy with your answer."

I secretly worried that I'd overstepped the mark but to my surprise he reacted calmly.

"You make a fair point John. I'll have to think about what you've said and discuss it with management. I'll get back to you soon with my answer."

Days later, he called me to his office and, as I sat in front of him, a thousand thoughts flashed through my mind. Would he send me back to Estcourt? He sat back and crossed his arms.

"We have decided to double your salary."

My heart pumped, surely I'd misheard. I let the news sink in and then a feeling of elation hit me. I still wouldn't be in the super-tax bracket but however little I was earning, by doubling it I'd taken a massive leap forward toward financial independence.

It didn't take long for the novelty to wear off and I became used to my newly found wealth. An uneasy mood had begun to take over as I looked at my older colleagues struggling with their bond repayments and it disturbed me when they told me how difficult it was for them to make ends meet. I had none of these financial constraints to weigh me down, but many of the salesmen were locked into the company and they considered the pension they'd get at sixty-five to be more important than the job itself.

I shuddered at the thought of grinding along for the next forty years creeping slowly up the corporate ladder and getting increases in line with the years that I spent with the company. It would be fair to say that I'd become disillusioned with my job and so, after nearly seven years, I tendered my resignation.

Shell had been good to me. I'd learned a lot, but I was ready for change. Sue and I were married and we moved to Johannesburg, where I took up a position with Muller & Phipps.

Muller & Phipps

Chapter 6

Learning the game

I joined Muller & Phipps in 1965 as a junior manager in charge of marketing services. The first few weeks were strange because after so many years at Shell I found that I needed to adjust to a whole new culture.

The company was established by Messrs Muller and Phipps, two American entrepreneurs who recognized that an opportunity existed to market and distribute consumer products. Since its founding, Muller & Phipps had grown into the largest organization of its kind in the world and its tentacles stretched across the globe. By the time I joined them, they were represented in forty-two countries. Although the company had expanded into a multi-million-dollar operation, it remained in the hands of the Muller family until the death of Muller. Following his death, control passed into the hands of the New York-based Phipps family.

We had the sole South African distribution rights for a range of products as diverse as Horlicks, Marmite, 3M, Tampax, Max Factor, Kelloggs, Klim, Richardson Vicks, and Oil of Olay and my role was to analyze the marketing and sales data. I soon ascertained that in spite of Muller & Phipps' size, they didn't possess a very sophisticated marketing or research system. My days at Shell served me in good stead because I had been taught the value of systematic and detailed research.

Unless you possess detailed statistical knowledge about your market and have information about your target market, or how your opposition operates, and how you can effectively measure performance, it is like going into battle without a sword.

There were gaping holes in the systems, so I set about introducing stricter controls to evaluate and measure the performance of the company sales force. I wanted to find out how effective their calls were and how frequently our customers purchased our products.

Armed with this important information, I set about formulating a grid system to help me establish where our strongest customer base was, how much they were spending and how often our salesmen should visit them. With this last piece of the jigsaw in place we were able to implement a strategic plan and soon we had the most potent and cost-effective consumer product sales force in the country.

With such a well-oiled sales machine we were able to sweep the opposition aside and we added NCD (National Co-operative Dairies) who also manufactured Clover Milk and allied products, and Cremora to our distribution portfolio. We expanded rapidly until we covered every corner of South Africa and our sales force burgeoned to over a hundred and fifty highly motivated professionals. Reckett & Coleman invited us to handle many of their lines and, by the time I left Muller & Phipps thirteen years later, we had grown into South Africa's second largest distributor of consumer products. Every aspiring executive needs a mentor to take them under their wing—in my case this was Dan da Costa. He eventually rose to become senior executive vice-president based in the United States, but he started on the bottom rung as a salesman and diligently worked his way through the ranks in South Africa.

For a number of years, he held the post of managing director in South Africa but his outstanding talents inevitably saw him move to the United States and he ended his career as the company number two. I owe much of what I learned about marketing techniques and how to foster good customer relations to Dan's help and guidance. He was without a shadow of doubt the finest marketer and most eloquent communicator that I have ever come across.

Those early days exposed me to a completely different side of business. Cussens, the makers of soap products such as Imperial Leather, were one of several companies which we represented that maintained a presence in South Africa, but had no staff or manufacturing infrastructure of their own. Instead Cussens entrusted every facet of the manufacture, marketing, distribution and sale of their products to Muller & Phipps.

We arranged the manufacture of their soap and talcum powder at a factory in Pietermaritzburg and contracted the packaging material to a Boksburg company. We also planned their advertising campaigns and managed their budget. This total operational responsibility provided one of the first examples of outsourcing in South Africa. The early success of this type of operation led to more and more international companies entrusting us to do the same for them.

I was in at the ground floor when Muller & Phipps initiated this method of total product and company management and it followed that I was rapidly exposed to a broad range of new activities. I learned how to plan manufacturing schedules, manage a national sales force, and supervise marketing and advertising expenditure.

All the major advertising agencies were hungrily eyeing Muller & Phipps. They were targeting us because it was common knowledge that we were spending huge sums of money on advertising and that we were controlling the budgets for many of our clients' campaigns.

I had only been with the company for a few months when Tony Snowden, the marketing manager, invited me to join him for an advertising agency lunch. I tagged along with Tony, excited at the thought of meeting a bunch of creative types and account executives. As we walked into the room, he was greeted like royalty and he clearly enjoyed the attention. Tony wielded considerable clout because he was the main decision-maker when it came to allocating our advertising budget. Over the years he'd established quite a reputation and he exuded self-assurance although, privately, many people in the advertising world thought that that he was self-opinionated, pompous and rather arrogant.

There was nothing that flattered Tony more than when he was the centre of any conversation and he enjoyed holding court on just about any subject. During lunch there was a lull in the conversation and silence descended as Tony, the elder statesman, began to hold forth about the importance of remembering people's names. The assembled guests, when he began pontificating, hung on to every word.

When he had the stage he said, "When I was younger I could never remember names. I used to meet people but I found that although I could remember their faces, their names slipped my memory. I worked out an amazingly simple solution. Let me show you what I mean because my technique is so easy and it works every time. I'll give you an example. Many of you only met for the first time today and you were introduced but I bet you can't recall many of each other's names. In fact you probably forgot their names within minutes. None of us are wearing name tags but I'll demonstrate how I developed my technique."

The audience sat riveted to their chairs, thirty pairs of eyes were focused on Tony waiting to seize on his pearls of wisdom.

"Take this fellow just here."

He pointed to a man sitting close to him.

"This is what you do. Can you see what big ears he has? That's the first thing I noticed when we were introduced so I fixed it in my mind. Ears start with 'E' and so does Errol which is his first name. You see how easy it is? He tells me his surname and I immediately see that he has a prominent nose. That's an 'N' for Nowell. I will never forget. Believe me, once practised, this method never fails and people think that you are terrific."

Errol looked down sheepishly, too embarrassed to respond. There was a stunned silence before the conversation slowly began again. I was down at the far end of the table and the guy next to me said, "John, I know that your boss told us that it works every time, but we all know 'Errol' well and we all call him Peter Tindall!"

Muller & Phipps landed the sole agency for an amazing product from Israel. It was called Tuffy and came in several different flavours. All you had to do was add water and you could make a milkshake. The packaging created an instant appeal because it came in a plastic container shaped like a tumbler. It was a natural for our market.

I was in charge of penetrating new markets and promoting our products so Tuffy was a golden opportunity to use my imagination. I set up meetings with several of our largest customers.

I figured that the best way to get the message across was to demonstrate how easy Tuffy was to make and then get them to try it out for themselves. I armed myself with samples of each flavour and a flask of ice-cold water.

I'd sit in front of the buyer and demonstrate how to make this miracle milkshake drink.

It wasn't hard to get Tuffy into all the major national food retailers such as Pick 'n Pay, Checkers, Trevenna, and Spar and all of them were enthusiastic about the product.

However, try as I may I couldn't convince the buyer responsible for placing the orders for OK Bazaars in Eastern and Northern Transvaal (now Mpumalanga and Limpopo respectively). Her name was Bertha and no matter how persuasive I was or whatever logical argument I put forward, she simply wouldn't budge. She wouldn't even try Tuffy out.

Tony Snowden also believed that he was a super-salesman and that he could overcome any buyer resistance. Next time I went to OK Bazaars, Tony came along. He was determined he wasn't leaving without an order. Tony went into his sales pitch while Bertha sat stony faced. When he finished he asked how many she'd like to take. Bertha was unmoved and replied, "I've told him," pointing to me, "and now I'm telling you. I am not interested in the product, I don't like it and I will never order it. Please don't pester me anymore."

Tony's persuasive abilities had been nipped in the bud but he was not to be thwarted. "I don't see how you can possibly say that you won't stock it before you have tasted the product. It is an absolute winner and everybody is going wild about Tuffy!

"Just try it once. Forget the fact that you think it's no good—your customers will love it. If you try it and you are still not impressed we won't bother you again."

Bertha finally relented with great reluctance and ill grace.

"What flavour can I make for you?" I asked.

She shrugged and shook her head impatiently, "Just get on with it. I don't care what flavour you give me because I can't stand milkshakes."

My heart sunk and I knew that it would be an uphill battle. Tony came to my rescue and said, "Make Bertha a lime-flavoured one, John. People are buying it like there's no tomorrow."

I felt like a magician at a kids' party as I theatrically poured two spoonfuls into the drinking container and topped it up with ice-cold water from the thermos flask. Tony took the mixture from me and put the cap on with a flourish. I had to stop myself from saying abracadabra and waving my magic wand.

Tony, forever the showman, turned to Bertha and said, "You see how simple it is; all you have to do to make a perfect drink is to give it a good shake for twenty seconds or so."

Tony began to shake the mixture vigorously but within seconds the cap flew off. I looked on mortified as the desk, walls and, worst of all, Bertha's beehive hairstyle were drenched in a thick green sludge. She wiped the mixture from her eyes and made a vain attempt to mop the lime-green milkshake off her light-brown polyester suit. I waited for the tirade but Bertha gave us a look that froze us to our chairs and stalked out of the room.

"I suppose that means Bertha won't be taking Tuffy" I said, somewhat at a loss for words.

The door flew open and a flushed assistant indicated that we had about five seconds to get out if we valued our lives. It was the last time that Tony ever went anywhere where I'd failed to close a sale.

Chapter 7

Climbing the ladder

I'd been progressing well during the seven years I'd been with the company when out of the blue the general manager resigned. I saw it as an opportunity to step up even though it meant that I'd be jumping a couple of grades. I was ambitious and harboured ideas of getting an international posting. I knew that competition would be fierce but I held high hopes because my great mentor Dan da Costa was flying out to South Africa as part of the team tasked with appointing a new general manager. I was certain that I was ready but my hopes were dashed when they appointed an outsider.

I was bitterly disappointed because I believed that I had all the experience and qualities that the job demanded. I asked Dan why I had been overlooked. He took me aside and broke the news as gently as he could under the circumstances.

"John, you were a great candidate and we've earmarked you for big things in Muller & Phipps but right now you are just too young for such a senior position. Hang in there in a couple of years you'll get the promotion that you deserve."

I hated the thought that I'd been passed over just because I was too young and I found it difficult to accept. However, as luck would have it, it hardly mattered because in less than a year the new general manager didn't work out and Dan once again came out to South Africa. Yet again I applied and this time he made his choice almost immediately. He called me to his office and I knew what he was about to tell me from the huge beam on his face. "Congratulations—you're still a young man but we have complete faith in your ability to be number two in the company. Now run with it."

I threw myself into the new challenge and set about putting my personal stamp on all facets of sales, manufacturing, packaging, distribution, marketing, and public relations—in fact everything except finance which was outside my responsibility. At age thirty-two I'd managed to climb two rungs and suddenly the national sales manager and the marketing manager were reporting to me. At first it seemed strange because only days before I'd been their junior. It must have been tough for them because they were both twenty years older than me, but they accepted and supported me well.

After my appointment a close friend and colleague, Tim McCarthy, and I used to go for a drink after work to chat over the day's events. Our favourite watering hole was the Dawson's Hotel just around the corner from our offices in Innes Chambers. We'd go there most evenings while we waited for the rush-hour traffic to die down. Tim was a pretty calm sort of guy and the only time that I really worried was when he'd been drinking rum. For some reason it made him fairly aggressive.

Early one evening when we walked into the upstairs lounge bar it was pretty quiet and there were just a couple of English chaps about the same age as us sitting at the bar. Some time later a young Afrikaans couple walked in, obviously killing time before going to the movies just across the road. The man was wearing a charcoal-coloured suit and tie. I noticed that he had white socks and black shoes.

The English guys began to poke fun at his socks and they went on and on until the joke started to wear thin. Tim got up to go to the gents, but on the way he stopped briefly to pass a comment to them. When he came back I asked him what he said.

"I just told them that I didn't like what they were saying about that guy's socks. I said that if they carried on I would take it personally."

A couple of minutes later one of them passed another offensive remark. Tim got up without saying a word and walked over to the bar. He tapped one of them on the shoulder and followed up with a right cross that knocked him clean off his stool.

He sprawled on the floor with blood pouring from a cut on his mouth. Tim said tersely, "I think it would be a good idea if you left now."

His friend didn't seem inclined to try his luck with Tim. He helped his friend up, propped him up against the bar, put a handkerchief over his mouth to staunch the bleeding and staggered out. Tim turned to the couple, apologized for the ill-mannered behaviour and insisted on paying for their drinks. It typified Tim's sense of fair play.

Chapter 8

Something for the weekend

It was a time of growth and our South African client base expanded. I swiftly introduced several large accounts, among them Elite Milk Powder, Ultramel, Duracell, Ronson, Tabasco and Gladwrap. Many international companies were anxious to establish a toehold in the country and while they concentrated on building their public image, they asked us to look after all other aspects of their business.

Julius Schmidt was one of our smaller clients but nonetheless we'd managed to jockey them into second place in the condom stakes. It was a time when nobody talked about condoms and it was very much a nod-and-a-wink type of product. You certainly didn't find them on supermarket shelves and men or errant schoolboys were somewhat embarrassed when they had to buy them. Pharmacies kept them hidden and the old clichéd phrase that was supposedly uttered by a smirking assistant, "Something for the weekend, sir?" was simply not true. In reality most men sidled up to a male assistant, slapped fifty cents on the counter and hoped that they'd get what they wanted and that their mumbled words wouldn't result in being handed a packet of headache tablets instead.

One day I received a letter from Julius Schmidt enquiring why, in spite of our success with the product, we never ordered anything other than the standard-sized pack of regular condoms. I was amazed to learn from their brochure that far from the Henry Ford concept of cars only being available in black, condoms could indeed be anything other than white! They sent dozens of samples of condoms of every conceivable hue as well as ribbed versions and told me that in America men often colour-coordinated their sexual activities!

With my condom education rounded out, I was keen to pass on my newfound knowledge to the sales force. I called the sales team to a Friday afternoon meeting to launch the coloured condoms. Most of the salesmen were young and virile and they embraced the product with considerable enthusiasm. I wanted to test the market so I said to them, "Go away with a sample of each and check out what your wives or girlfriends like best. If we know this we can advise pharmacies what ratio of each colour they should stock."

When the chatter died down I said, "That's not all. Julius Schmidt wants us to try out a new line called Last Long. It is a cream that you put on your penis before you have sex and it helps you prolong your lovemaking. Take a sample with you and let me know how it works out."

This new product was not greeted as positively as the coloured condoms and all the salesmen except one were too macho to admit that they'd ever need such a thing. I concluded that Last Long wouldn't catch on and stuck the samples in a display cabinet. Next time that I went to look for them they were gone. We never found out who took them but somebody's wife must have been wearing a permanent smile!

Graham Medcalf, a great friend of mine, was the lone salesman bold enough to admit to using the product. One evening we were invited for dinner and Rhona, his wife, tackled me. She was tiny, less than fifty kilos, but she certainly punched her weight. She looked at me menacingly and said, "I haven't found out what you gave to Graham but if you ever give it to him again I'll murder you. He may have had a great time but I was driven bonkers!" Graham subsequently left Muller & Phipps and helped found Hunt Lascaris & Medcalf, an advertising agency that went on to become one of South Africa's most dynamic and creative. Graham moved to New Zealand and I often wonder if he recalls the time that he test-drove such a revolutionary product.

Having successfully introduced the new product, I was confronted by a marketing dilemma. The price of Julius Schmidt condoms was twice as much as that of our local competitor. I accepted that because Julius Schmidt was imported, it followed that it would be more expensive. However, retailers didn't see any good reason why they should give sales effort to it; the sales team said that they couldn't get pharmacists to buy extra product that did the same job as the local brand at half the cost.

I gave this a great deal of thought and finally the penny dropped. I trained the sales team to say to pharmacists: "Don't worry about the price because men will always need to buy them. Perhaps you'll sell fewer of our condoms but every one you do, seeing that they are double the price, will mean that you make double the profit."

It seemed logical, but the fact remained that pharmacists still had to convince their customers to shell out more than they were accustomed to paying. We used basic psychology and our salesmen showed their customers how to address the problem. When a customer came into the shop they were taught to say, "If you want the best why don't you try this new brand from the USA?"

The customers wanted to avoid getting into a lengthy debate in front of other customers. All they wanted to do was purchase their condoms as quickly as possible and hurry out of the place. With this simple bit of salesmanship we cracked the market and in no time our sales rocketed.

I was on my way back from Cape Town with a colleague one evening after spending an exhausting couple of days launching a new product to the sales team. As we stood at the baggage carousel I saw a familiar face. I wracked my brains to remember who he was, because when you meet somebody out of context you can't always put a name to a face. It soon hit me—it was Herman Aijello, a guy I hadn't seen since my schooldays. He was a brilliant maths and science student, one of those types that goes on to carve out careers in industry.

In those days the business dress code was extremely formal and I was wearing a dark suit and tie. Herman looked as if he'd been in the bush for weeks. He was dressed in dirty khaki trousers, his soiled shirt was sweat stained and he hadn't shaved for days. My first reaction was to ignore him, but he spotted me and made his way over to us. The last thing I wanted at that moment was to introduce this dishevelled, unkempt chap to my colleague. Herman smiled warmly and thrust out his hand.

"How are you John, long time no see. What are you doing with yourself nowadays?"

I didn't want to prolong the exchange but I also didn't want to appear rude. "Hi Herman, I didn't see you on the flight."

"I wasn't on your flight."

"I thought ours was the last flight?"

"I wasn't on a scheduled airline."

"You mean you were on a charter flight?"

"Not exactly, I came in on a private plane."

"That's great. Do you have a pilot's licence?"

"No. My pilot flew me in."

"Have you been spending a couple of days in the bush?"

He let out a deep belly laugh, threw his head back, and replied, "Fat chance of that! I'm rushed off my feet at present. My company has just got a massive contract to build the Natal South Coast highway."

It was a sobering lesson. I had thought that I was too important to be seen talking to him but, meanwhile, he could have bought and sold me a thousand times over! My father's words about humility and his philosophy about equality came back to haunt me.

Chapter 9

The price of success

During my time at Muller & Phipps my marriage ended abruptly, and I was left to raise my two children. At the time Delia was two and my son Sean a little over three years old. Life took on new meaning and from leading a fairly orderly existence chaos prevailed.

I desperately wanted to put things back on the rails and I increasingly began to lean on Glynnis, my personal assistant at Muller & Phipps. My frequent trips out of town meant that I had to rely on other parents to pick up the children and ferry them around. Often on occasions when people let me down I had to excuse myself from an important meeting, rush across town, and drop them off with my maid before dashing back to work. It was a nightmare of epic proportions.

Whenever I had to leave Johannesburg for a few nights, Glynnis would move into my house and take over the role of nanny. She got the children ready for school, made sure that they got proper meals and tucked them up in bed. The situation was far from ideal and my conscience began to prick me. It was fortunate too that at this point my friend Tim McCarthy came to stay with me.

Leading from the Front

I was in New York on my annual trip to do the rounds of our various customers across the United States, from Minneapolis to Los Angeles, San Francisco and Washington, before beginning my schedule of head office meetings in New York. On the Friday morning I had hardly unpacked when I got a call from Bill Phipps.

"Hi John, welcome to New York. Can I interest you in a round of golf tomorrow?"

I was caught off guard because although Bill knew that I played golf, we'd never actually played together. "Yes, I'd love to but I didn't come prepared. I don't have any kit or clubs with me."

Bill was insistent. "Don't worry about that. If you want to play I'll have my chauffeur collect you from your hotel at two tomorrow."

I thought that I had a fair grasp of how wealthy people lived from the few rich people I knew in Johannesburg, but they were in the nursery school league compared with Bill. His mansion in Engelwood was more palatial than anything I'd ever seen.

We drove over to the Engelwood Country Club and went straight to the pro shop. I was surprised to see that a choice of trousers, shirts, socks and shoes all in my size had already been laid out for me. I picked out what I needed and we went to change.

"Let's hit a few balls before we tee off," Bill suggested, heading toward the driving range.

I was used to practising with pretty scuffed, used balls and so I was a little taken aback to see a neat little triangle containing fifty or so brand-new balls. I immediately knew that this was no ordinary club and that members were extremely well heeled.

The course was immaculately manicured. I could imagine an army of greenkeepers trimming the fairways with nail scissors at dawn each morning. We played a very relaxed round; we were pretty evenly matched and I was happy not to have embarrassed myself. When we got back to the change rooms a valet handed my clothes to me and I tried hard to suppress a smile. My shirt and trousers had been pressed and I could see my reflection in the toecaps of my shoes!

Bill warned me that we'd be having dinner at the club after golf and, knowing that Americans are often rather formal, I'd had the foresight to bring a jacket and tie.

Waiters wearing dinner jackets and white gloves hovered around the table attentively and in company with Bill's guests, who were clearly also very well off, we enjoyed a fabulous meal and the finest imported wines. I was intrigued to see that nobody was presented with the bill at the end of the meal and so when we got back to Bill's house I broached the subject as delicately as I could.

"Bill, I don't want to appear nosy but that wonderful meal—does it get put on your account?"

Bill was the consummate gentleman and didn't appear phased at my rather bold question. He said, "I don't exactly know how to put this without sounding too elitist. Englewood Country Club actually has relatively few members and we try to keep it that way. We want it to be exclusive. The way it works out is that each year we tot up the entire cost of running the club and then we split the total amount equally among the members. If you play once or a hundred times or if you eat and entertain your friends every day or never, it makes no difference."

I mentally tried to calculate what sort of money would be involved but it seemed so overwhelming.

"That's incredible, but why would you ever want to do it? Don't you think that it could be unfair to some members if people start abusing the system?"

Bill stunned me with his reply, "I can't even begin to put a price on what it means when I mention to my friends and business acquaintances that I'm a member at Engelwood. We don't encourage people to join; in fact membership is via invitation only."

Friends, sport, relationships

Chapter 10

Giving life texture

Tim McCarthy was one of my close friends and I shared a number of houses with him over the years. As my children grew and needed to move to new schools, I had to move house. So wherever we went, Tim came along.

Tim was a pretty smooth operator with the ladies. As some of our houses we rented were quite fancy, Tim loved to bring girls home to impress them with all the gizmos such as heated towel rails or under-floor heating. He used to say that a conducted tour of the house worked far better for him than expensive aftershave!

One of the houses we rented was at the top of Northcliff Hill. We lived there for a number of years and every time we had ladies around for dinner we relied on our wonderful maid, Momsie, to turn on the full works. She knew exactly what to do. Momsie bought out the candlesticks and laid flowers on the table and dragged out our best crockery and glassware.

If his partner for the evening had been bowled over by the glamour of the house and the meal, Tim would turn to her and say, "You can move in with us if you want. It will only cost you seventy rand a month! We've got a couple of spare bedrooms."

I always chuckled when I heard this line because Tim was paying seventy rand a month toward the rent. He thought that he'd found the perfect solution to defray his expenses!

One Friday evening Tim and I were entertaining two alluring young ladies. I was busy preparing drinks when there was a knock at the door. I went to answer it and I was confronted by a girl that Tim had given the sales talk to the previous week. She smiled broadly and began to haul her suitcase into the entrance hall.

I asked her to wait while I called Tim. He handled the situation with complete aplomb. He introduced her to our two guests and hustled her into one of the bedrooms.

When Tim came back to our guests you could cut the atmosphere with a knife. The evening deteriorated rapidly and the table conversation was punctuated by long silences. Not even the crystal glasses seemed to help this time. Our guests left early.

Next morning Tim sheepishly had to explain to our new lodger that she would have to leave. Tim drove her back and it was the last time that he ever tried to subsidize his rent money with his seduction routine.

A while later Tim met Gail, a wonderful woman who was his match on every level. She was intelligent, well educated and was truly a chip off the old block. Tim was absolutely smitten by her and they were married not long after they met.

Gail's father had achieved a degree of notoriety for his outspoken views while he was editor of the *Rhodesian Herald*. He was a bitter opponent of Ian Smith and, as a consequence, his entire editorial had to be vetted before the newspaper went to print. He retaliated by leaving huge blanks where any offending articles had been censored. He was finally deported and returned to his home in Scotland.

Although Tim was a dyed in the wool South African, he was troubled by the government's apartheid policies and saw little hope for the future. He left the country and moved to St Andrews in Scotland to be near to Gail's father. As the years passed we lost touch and to my knowledge he has never been back to South Africa.

As I began to reassess my status as a bachelor my thoughts turned to the opposite sex once more. I realized that, except for the ladies who had come to the house for dinner, I'd become out of touch with how to meet single women.

I cast around for something that would make me appear more glamorous and attractive. Flying seemed to fit the bill and I rather hoped that if I was able to get a pilot's licence that my exploits in the cockpit would offer me something to impress women with. With this primary aim I decided to enrol for flying lessons.

At the time Baragwanath airfield boasted the largest collection of Tiger Moths in the world. I pitched up there one Saturday morning and I was assigned to one of the many instructors who were going to show me how to pilot a Cessna 150. This aircraft is a very basic machine although due to my somewhat limited grasp of anything technical the dials and gauges appeared daunting. I was shown how to do a pre-flight check which involved little more than pushing a button on the side and checking whether there was fuel in the tank. I did a few flights over the next couple of weeks with a number of different instructors but never got the same instructor twice running. There was certainly no time to develop any relationship with any one of them.

I logged about twelve hours before being allowed to go solo. The day finally arrived although I didn't know it and I was joined by another instructor whom I'd never seen before. He led me to an aircraft that seemed strange and not at all like the Cessna 'FDI' that I was used to. I climbed into the cockpit next to the instructor and I was mildly alarmed to find that the five gauges that I was familiar with appeared to be juxtaposed. I pressed on regardless as I didn't want to alarm the instructor. I had learned that take-off was fairly straightforward whereas landing was a different kettle of fish. Each instructor had a preference either to make a long slow descent or come in faster and steeper. Anyway I did a few circuits and bumps to put in the flying time and then I made an almost perfect landing.

We taxiied down the runway and as we came to a standstill the instructor turned to me and said, "There you go!" Only minutes later did it occur to me that he thought that I had already gone solo!

My flying exploits didn't last long. My fist solo flight was hair–raising. I didn't know that the plane was fitted with a Klaxon horn that went off when you hit stalling speed. It happened when I was preparing to land the aircraft which was about three metres above the tarmac. I was so startled that I just dropped the aircraft from about three metres and bounced down the runway onto the grass. I was in shock and shaking like a leaf. I decided that I would quit while I was ahead and draw a veil over my career as a pilot.

Muller & Phipps

Chapter 11

Encounter with big brother

In 1973 I received a phone call that shook me to the core.

"Good morning Mr Barry. I am Colonel van Rensburg from the South African police force in John Vorster Square. Perhaps it would be a good idea for both of us if we had a little chat in my office. Can you make it tomorrow morning?"

An icy chill gripped me. John Vorster Square had frequently been in the news for all the wrong reasons and all too often detainees who were suspected of subversion had mysteriously fallen to their death from a tenth-floor window. I tried to recover my composure and agreed to meet him.

"Can you give me some idea as to why you want to speak to me?"

"I'm afraid that I can't discuss it over the phone. All I can say is that it's very important that we meet. I'll see you at eleven."

I went to John Vorster Square with great trepidation. I announced myself to the receptionist on duty and waited until a police constable came to fetch me. It immediately struck me that the tight cordon of security I'd heard about was no myth. The elevator only went to the fifth floor and then one exited and caught another lift that operated only from the sixth floor upward. That explains a lot, I thought to myself. Anyone being interrogated on the upper floors could never escape.

I was ushered into Colonel van Rensburg's office and he motioned for me to take a seat opposite him. We exchanged pleasantries and he seemed charming and polished. He didn't reflect the dour, iron-fisted image most of us had about the security police. He didn't appear in a hurry to get to the point of our meeting and it made me nervous.

"Tell me colonel, what did you want to see me about?"

He was not drawn into a direct answer but instead said, "Mr Barry, I believe that you are a British citizen. We have made enquiries about where you went to school and now I'd like to know why you have never applied to be a South African citizen after living for all these years in the Republic."

This line of questioning was beginning to unnerve me and I thought that I'd better be careful how I answered. "I love this country and would never think of living anywhere else but the government apartheid policies trouble me."

He fixed me with a stare but didn't respond directly. Instead he continued to probe and then listened to my answers in a calm and controlled way.

"Colonel van Rensburg, I have told you my life story but you still haven't given me any reason why you wanted me to come here."

"I will tell you when you have told me a little more about yourself."

I could sense that my answers were branding me as a liberal-thinking white. I must have seemed just the type of person that the security police were trying to clamp down on.

"My father often worked abroad and so I have been at school in Egypt, Pakistan, India and Burma. Colonel van Rensburg, all this has meant that the race and colour of people doesn't concern me."

"Yes, we checked on your background and it seems to be in line with what you have told me today."

"So now, Colonel van Rensburg, can you please tell me why I'm here?"

His reply left me speechless and churned my stomach. "Mr Barry, we have a very reliable report that says you have threatened to assassinate the Prime Minister."

"I may well disassociate myself from the distasteful apartheid policies but what you've just said is too ridiculous for words. The report is a pack of lies. Who made this outrageous report? I'd really like to know."

He said, "This information is confidential. We don't ever disclose our source, but I repeat that it is totally reliable."

I was spitting mad and I hit back, "If I am supposed to be about to assassinate the Prime Minister, don't you think that I have a right to be told who reported me? I want to meet him face to face. Let him make his allegations and I will soon show you how absurd it is."

He studied me intently and he didn't answer for what seemed like minutes, "Mr Barry, after our little chat I don't think that you are the type to resort to violence. I am sorry to have bothered you. You should think hard about anyone who could have a grudge against you. Maybe an employee you've dismissed or something like that."

I left John Vorster Square mulling over what had been said. I couldn't possibly guess who would resort such measures to get at me. I didn't hear from Colonel van Rensburg again and I moved on with my life.

Over the course of the next week or two I forgot about this unsavoury incident. I was living alone at the time, before I was given custody of my children. I was working long hours and, usually, by the time I got back to my apartment in Craighall I just about had time to grab something to eat before falling into bed. My culinary skills didn't extend beyond opening a tin and warming the contents so, when I was hungry, I sometimes popped down to the local steakhouse to grab a bite.

One evening I got the distinct feeling that I was being followed in my car. I told myself not to become paranoid, but the memory of my interview at John Vorster Square made me jittery. I tried to check if I was imagining things, so I drove around aimlessly for fifteen minutes. There was no doubt I was being tailed. After leaving the steakhouse I returned home but I couldn't shake off the nagging feeling that I was under surveillance and, when I peeped out from behind the curtains, I could see the same unmarked car waiting under a tree. For the next four months, whenever I went out at whatever time, I was followed. Colonel van Rensburg was obviously not taking any chances. I considered calling him to ask when this nasty little charade would end. Then without warning the surveillance stopped and I began living normally again.

Chapter 12

Hard facts of business life

I revelled in the daily challenges of running Muller & Phipps. The company expanded and I was on a roll.

Toward the end of my tenure, Pick 'n Pay was emerging as a supermarket giant and, as they spread out across the country, the entire face of in-store merchandising began to change. As Pick 'n Pay steadily became more powerful, they slowly squeezed the manufacturers in a manner that their competitors such as Checkers never had. I believe to this day that their ruthless tactics have contributed to rapidly rising prices.

Before Pick 'n Pay started to dominate, manufacturers made bulk deliveries to the Checkers and OK Bazaars warehouses and the frequency was based on the quantity of their order. That was the way things were done and it was accepted by everyone until Pick 'n Pay began to employ bully-boy tactics in an attempt to gain an edge over other retailers.

Pick 'n Pay buyers began to demand deliveries of smaller quantities to individual stores more frequently and at the same or better prices than those of bulk deliveries made to their competitors. Those terms were onerous enough, but they also forced the suppliers to unpack their own stock onto the shelves. The inherent threat was that, unless they complied with their demands, Pick 'n Pay would stop doing business with them.

This development resulted in Muller & Phipps having to redeploy staff from our warehouse to pack shelves for Pick 'n Pay. It wasn't long before all supermarkets followed the trend and in doing so a huge new industry was spawned. Muller & Phipps were forced to make a heavy investment and in a short while we were employing around a hundred shelf-packers to perform the function. This new development meant that we had to absorb the cost of what was hitherto a supermarket expense.

It wasn't long before this became an established practice, and so I attempted to turn this negative trend into a business opportunity. Many manufactures only supplied Pick 'n Pay with one or two products and their resources were stretched to the limit. We offered these companies a shelf-stacking and distribution service.

It was fairly straightforward for us to merge the smaller suppliers' interests with ours. We employed more and more staff to supplement their demands and within months we had a team of three hundred and fifty employees packing shelves. We developed a scientific approach to this burgeoning business by logging and refining the frequency of our calls. Pick 'n Pay's excessive and unreasonable demands evolved into an entirely new shelf-packing business and one that Muller & Phipps developed into a profitable division.

The next logical step for us was to establish a team to handle in–store promotions. Promotions are an effective way of creating public awareness of various products by way of discount coupons or by encouraging shoppers to test-taste. It was relatively easy to expand into this new business as an extension to our other activities and at our peak we had more than a thousand full and part-time demonstrators on our payroll.

Muller & Phipps was expanding in all directions and our range of non-food and toiletries was snowballing. When we were searching for new products we found the USA to be a fertile hunting ground.

We secured the agency to represent Hammond Organs, Floresheim shoes and Dobbs Hats. Floresheim were acknowledged to be the Rolls Royce of shoes because they were extremely expensive and black South African men viewed owning a pair as the ultimate status symbol. At that time black South Africans weren't permitted by law to own homes in the suburbs and for most of them cars were far too expensive. Nonetheless, they needed an outward sign of their success and Floresheim shoes fitted the bill perfectly. A pair of Floresheim's were so highly prized that we deliberately created an air of exclusivity by limiting our distribution to a handful of outlets.

When we were appointed to represent Duracell batteries, we faced an uphill battle to market and sell a product that cost three times more than the established Eveready brand. Duracell batteries were imported and they had no track record in South Africa. Because they faced absolutely no competition, Eveready had captured 100% of the local market. We thought long and hard about how we could use our experience to overcome the problem. After all, years before we managed to turn the market round with Schmidt condoms but this was subtly different. Condoms were sold in pharmacies whereas batteries were sold by all and sundry.

Duracell was a far better product than Eveready and the unique selling point was its extended lifespan. We launched a campaign based on the fact that Duracell batteries lasted six times longer than Eveready. Even though Duracell batteries cost twice as much as Eveready it was such a powerful message that our sales took off. Even today this powerful slogan is still being used in the company advertising.

Dominance in any market can be double jeopardy and so it proved. Retailers were irritated because hitherto there was no opposition battery product to use as a lever against Eveready when they tried to negotiate rebates. Duracell were the new boys on the block and the supermarket chains took the opportunity to put Eveready to the wall by ordering Duracell. The rest is history and Duracell swiftly became a household name in South Africa.

Chapter 13

It's not inside—it's on top

One of our biggest coups was the successful launch of Cremora.

In the mid-1970s we were invited to handle the distribution and marketing of Borden products, yet another American manufacturer. They made a range of food products including Klim, a reconstituted milk powder and Cremora, a coffee creamer. Nobody in South Africa, and not least, those of us at Muller & Phipps, had any idea of what exactly a coffee creamer was! Therein lay the marketing puzzle.

Supermarkets are notoriously twitchy about giving up shelf space to a product that doesn't increase their turnover. A manufacturer has to convince the buyer that his new brand of soap powder or baked beans will lead to higher sales rather than just dilute the sale of the brands that they already stocked. Perhaps major marketers such as Unilever or Nestlé have an easier ride, but it is still difficult to push a new line into a saturated market.

When we showed Cremora to supermarket buyers we introduced an entirely new terminology—'coffee creamer'. The concept had instant appeal, but we still had to figure out how to get the message across to housewives.

Cremora was a marketing dream because it had novelty value and had absolutely no competition. We called in the sales team and brainstormed the plus factors. It soon became clear that the selling points were that you didn't have to refrigerate it and it didn't make your coffee cold when you added it.

There was no doubt that it was a product that would appeal to consumers in the higher-income groups. Although it was a relatively small segment of the market it was also highly lucrative. We also realized that being *parava* it could be used by orthodox Jews on occasions where milk was not permitted.

To reinforce the campaign each salesman was presented with a replica of a milk churn and armed with the simple message.

'Cremora—its milk in a different form.'

The supermarkets embraced Cremora with enthusiasm and ordered in quantities that far exceeded our expectations. Our shelf-packers and salesmen were instructed to pack it between the two most popular coffee brands. We hoped that our cinema advertising launch would trigger housewives to reach for Cremora whenever they bought their coffee.

I was disturbed when letters from disgruntled consumers began to drop on our mat. They weren't complaining about the product. They just couldn't find it in the supermarket! They had seen the advertisement, liked the idea and were then frustrated because they couldn't find it on their local supermarket shelf.

Orders dried up and I couldn't explain why so I went on a tour of twenty stores. To my amazement I couldn't find it either!

I confronted one of the store managers. "You bought several cases of Cremora but sales are shocking. Our customers say that they want to buy Cremora but they can't find it next to the coffee. Show me where you put it."

He replied, "We don't put it with the coffee. It's a coffee creamer, like milk."

I said, "Where do you put it then?"

He led me to the fridge and triumphantly showed me how he'd given it ample exposure among the cartons of milk.

In store after store I discovered that they'd been doing the same thing. We'd committed a blunder in telling store people that Cremora was "milk in another form". The problem was exacerbated because most consumers still had their milk delivered to their doorstep. We'd shot ourselves in the foot. We'd delivered huge quantities to the supermarkets and we'd created consumer demand but because the product was hard to find we weren't penetrating the market.

I called my great friend Graham de Villiers who had created the original consumer advertising campaign. He was the managing director of De Villiers & Schoenveldt and he possessed a great creative and marketing mind. When we met I outlined our problem and discussed the need for a solution to help us put Cremora back on track.

He came up with a slogan that was nothing short of genius. It was so simple yet mightily effective and thirty years on it is still used and is probably the most quoted payoff line of all time.

'It's not inside—it's on top!'

What started as a marketing disaster ended as a dazzling success story. When Nestlé bought out Borden I donated my original promotional milk churn to their managing director for their museum. Hopefully it will remind people of the early days of a product that has now become a household name.

Chapter 14

Dancing with Pick 'n Pay

I took marketing and product launches in my stride but my life became complicated when Pick 'n Pay started exerting pressure on the market.

I had personally dealt with Raymond Ackerman from the time when he first purchased four stores in Cape Town. I watched him from the wings as he turned his low-key operation into an empire. Raymond Ackerman is unquestionably a marketing genius. I have admiration for many innovations he brought to South African supermarkets. His self-promotion skills are legendary and he has created a personal aura. Housewives view him as a knight in shining armour, a man who rides a white horse and goes to battle on their behalf.

I recall the time when I invited an exclusive group of South Africa's elite retailers to a conference in Dallas hosted by Borden Foods. Raymond Ackerman was among the guests and I welcomed the opportunity of learning more about his marketing philosophy. I questioned him about it and I vividly remember his answer and it has stuck in my mind. The concept is so blindingly obvious but it took Ackerman to put it into words.

"I operate an island of loss in a sea of profit."

He went on to explain that housewives knew to the cent how much twenty staple items cost, for example. They bought things like milk and bread most days and these were price-sensitive items.

"We make absolutely certain that we aren't undercut on any of these lines. We make our profit by marking up things that consumers don't buy as often and don't keep tabs on their exact cost."

Yes, Raymond Ackerman is both a marketing genius and a true gentleman. Regrettably his henchmen at the next level down with whom I had dealings over the years were unquestionably some of the most ruthless people I have ever conducted business with. I was disillusioned to discover that many of them were totally devoid of subtlety, lacked charm and common courtesy and in my opinion operated in an unethical manner.

I still cannot accept or condone the unscrupulous methods they employed to drive the deals for their organization. While I may understand their end goal, their steamroller tactics were distasteful, unpalatable and unacceptable to every supplier that I have ever known. Any supplier bold enough to stand up to their storm-trooping policies was simply squashed and if anyone got out of line Pick 'n Pay retaliated by refusing to stock their products.

Muller & Phipps carried a vast range of well-known and prominent products such as Cremora, Gladwrap and Marmite. To maintain the integrity of each brand it was essential that we represented the individual interests of each manufacturer whenever we visited a supermarket chain. I often met senior buyers to promote a product or to negotiate special offers. Competitions were very popular and they gave consumers the opportunity to win a luxury car or a of lounge suite by answering a simple question or pulling off a lucky bottle top. They proved to be a huge drawcard.

Pick 'n Pay began to adopt a different philosophy. They flew against convention and a very senior buyer told me in no uncertain terms, "We don't believe in prizes. We believe in prices. You will have to reduce your prices by whatever a car or holiday would cost. That's the way we are going." I didn't react but I absorbed the news and filed it in my memory bank.

A short time later I met Norman Leibov, a very senior Pick 'n Pay executive. My objective was to set up the same type of promotion that we'd successfully held with Checkers. I also wanted to propose another idea that would bring people into his stores. I sensed that he wasn't happy and I knew that he was well versed in what the opposition were doing. The success of the Checkers promotion was fresh in his mind and it probably rankled him. I had barely entered his office and pulled up a chair when he attacked me. "That promotion you've been doing with Checkers must have cost you a hell of a lot of money!"

I could guess what he was driving at but I refused to be deflected, "Yes, successful promotions always cost a lot."

Leibov was working himself into a frenzy and he raised his voice in anger, "I've pulled out the figures of what I think you would have sold and I've worked out how much that promotion must have cost. Now I want a backdated rebate on every case that we bought during this deal period. I want to get an amount equivalent to the cost of that promotion."

I was shaken but I knew that I had to stand my ground. "Norman, I'm sorry but what you've suggested is absolutely out of the question. We will set up a promotion for Pick 'n Pay later in the year using the exact product and the same terms. However, that's not why I came to see you today. I want to discuss an entirely different promotion."

But he was adamant and he became increasingly agitated. "I don't want to hear about promotions. Hear what I say. If you don't give me exactly what I want, you can forget about getting another order from Pick 'n Pay for any of your products!"

I was determined not to be bullied into doing what I knew was commercial suicide. "That's not reasonable or fair. You are threatening to punish every one of the suppliers that we represent. You know full well that because one supplier has upset you it doesn't give you a reason to penalize them all."

"I've made my point abundantly clear," he said. "It's in your hands so go away and think about it. Call me tomorrow when you have had time to mull over my words. Let me know when you agree to our terms."

I phoned him the next day and said, "Norman your proposal makes no sense and so I can't give you what you want."

Within a day he'd sent out a notice to every one of his store managers instructing them not to purchase any Muller & Phipps product.

It was the straw that almost broke the camel's back. I had endured a tempestuous relationship with him over the years and now it had reached rock bottom. I decided to write to Raymond Ackerman who by that time was no longer involved in the day-to-day operation of the business.

I outlined my discussion with Norman Leibov and I reasoned that a boycott of all our products was going to harm our clients and would also be to the detriment of his customers.

Raymond Ackerman chose not to respond to me but instead I received a call from Leibov and he was spitting mad. "You have the temerity to go over my head to Mr Ackerman. You think that you are very clever. Be warned, I will show you. You haven't heard the last from me!"

Almost a third of the products we represented were the brand leaders in their fields. It was an important marketing strategy in the Fast-Moving Consumer Goods (FMCG) business for stores to put the best-selling items at eye level. Slower-moving items were relegated to the lower shelves. As a consequence fast-moving products got more eye-level shelf space.

Leibov had obviously been reprimanded by Ackerman and hated having to eat humble pie. He'd been forced to reverse his decision but he was determined to wreak his revenge by cutting our shelf space and reducing our visibility. He did it by ordering our goods to be packed on the bottom shelves. It was the mean and vindictive act of a wounded man but for six weeks he inflicted significant damage to all our clients. Pick 'n Pay buyers wielded that kind of power and suppliers found it intimidating but we managed to survive this war of attrition. I breathed a sigh of relief when things returned to normal but it was a moral victory for us, as we had not been forced to compromise our principles.

When I finally left the industry I did so with many regrets. I'd met many fine people, developed great friendships, handled the marketing, advertising and launches of some wonderful products and had an exhilarating career but the moral bankruptcy of buyers like Norman Leibov left a bad taste in my mouth.

Before Pick 'n Pay muscled onto the scene, retailers accepted that they had to buy significant quantities in a single delivery to qualify for the keenest price. Pick 'n Pay broke the mould and demanded, and received, the lowest bulk price irrespective of whether they ordered one case or a hundred. All this led to manufacturers making thousands more deliveries. They had little option but to pass on their increased transport costs by increasing their prices to all other retailers and this had the effect of increasing consumer prices across the board.

Chapter 15

Turning point

Muller & Phipps South African operation grew quickly during the period that I was general manager and my success consequently led to a number of tempting job offers.

I rejected several approaches to move to head office in New York because my personal circumstances wouldn't allow it. I was bitterly disappointed when I had to turn down invitations to take up managing director opportunities in Hong Kong and Hawaii. The latter would have offered huge scope because the liquor industry was at the core of their business operations. Muller & Phipps owned the island's largest brewery and they also distilled sugar cane-based spirits. In my heart I would have relished moving to Hong Kong, but as a single parent I couldn't have coped without my South African support system.

My domestic infrastructure was running like clockwork. This was due in the main to Mopsie who was an absolute gem. I guess that one would refer to her as a maid but to me she was the brightest star in the firmament. She was a superb mother to the children and was, I suppose, what today would be labelled a home executive. She possessed the skills of a PA, valet, butler, cook and bottle-washer. The fridge was always stocked, my clothes were always pressed and the kids loved her. She was quite simply irreplaceable and though she never knew it she was the biggest reason why I never accepted an overseas posting.

On a personal level my career in Muller & Phipps was very satisfying. I loved the company, revelled in what I did, and liked and respected all the people around me. I relished the success I had in creating and bringing to fruition some of the visions I had developed for the company. I was buoyed by the promise that one day I would be appointed managing director.

There are few things in life more gratifying than receiving praise, particularly when you are young. I treasured the complimentary letters from Dan da Costa and the president, Bill Phipps. They heaped praise on me for the success that I'd bought to the South African company. They passed on the glowing reports they received from many of our major principals. Each year when I travelled to the United States I was hosted by Bill Phipps himself and he treated me like a king. It was more than sufficient for me. I enjoyed a generous package and I experienced a high level of job satisfaction. I assumed that when the incumbent managing director retired, I would be the natural heir to the throne.

My world was soon turned upside down.

Out of the blue I received a call from Len Gullan who owned a company called Admark Advertising, a medium sized agency. Len handled the advertising for several accounts that Muller & Phipps represented so we had quite a lot of common interest. He handled the Horlicks and Cussens accounts for me so I wasn't particularly surprised when he suggested meeting me for a drink. He quickly cut to the chase and to my utter amazement he invited me to join his company as group managing director. Only much later did I learn that the title was the grandest part of the deal!

Len Gullan painted a glowing picture of the three companies under Admark's umbrella. He explained that Admark Advertising was complemented by a small public relations agency. This company, Three Oaks, was managed by a highly capable, likeable and creative man named Robin Binkes. I was aware that Robin staged the first hot-air balloon race in South Africa and was instrumental in bringing international cricket tours to the country. The Gullan stable was completed with a small typesetting company with the rather bizarre name of Tinkle.

I was rather detached as I listened to his proposal. Finally he produced his coup de grâce.

"If you accept, I will offer you the chance to buy 25% of the entire business for no more than the net asset value."

As I contemplated his offer over the next few days it struck me that there was a gaping chasm between being an employee earning a generous salary package and owning equity in a company and thus having the chance to create true wealth.

For the first time I became acutely aware that what I really wanted to do with my life was own a stake in a business and work hard to increase its value. I came to the inevitable conclusion that however long I remained with Muller & Phipps I would never be invited to become a stakeholder. Although in time I'd be earning a fabulous salary, I'd never create wealth.

With a heavy heart and mixed feelings I tendered my resignation and agreed to join Admark. It was in many ways a leap of faith because after a glittering career spanning thirteen years I was about to relinquish an enviable job as number two in a successful company. I was about to exchange job satisfaction and a comfortable salary for an uncertain future in a minnow-sized company in a field that I barely understood.

I suppose that what tipped the scales and led me to take the decision to resign was the thought that ultimately I could become rich. Nonetheless I couldn't shake off the nagging feeling of guilt. I would be letting down those wonderful people such as Dan da Costa who had had faith in me and had helped me achieve many of my aspirations.

Admark

Chapter 16

A test of faith

When I resigned in June 1976 Muller & Phipps tried really hard to persuade me to stay.

A flurry of calls from New York only served to make me feel more awkward and as the days passed I began to doubt the wisdom of my decision. Some weeks later the managing director called me to his office.

"I have been asked by the guys in New York to chat to you. They don't want to lose you and they have decided to offer you a share of the profits and they'll also agree to up your salary."

I drew a deep breath. I knew that it was a make-or-break answer. If I cracked now I would probably be with Muller & Phipps for another twenty years.

"I have to say no. The offer is flattering and it's a more generous package than I'll be getting at Admark but I've thought about it for a long time. As you know the only reason I want to leave is because I've been offered the chance to build my own business. If I make a success of it I will have the opportunity to create real wealth."

Muller & Phipps were not ready to give up and they countered my flat refusal with yet another improved offer. This time I began to waver. I sat at my desk with a blank sheet of paper and began to list the all reasons to stay in the left column and all the disadvantages on the right. I weighted some of the more important points before adding them up but, in the end, I decided to leave.

Muller & Phipps were shaken because they'd been convinced that if they applied enough pressure I would crack. More importantly they worried because they didn't have any successor in mind. They hadn't given a moment's thought to grooming anyone to do my job as the senior management naturally assumed that I would stay with the company forever.

They pleaded with me to extend my notice period to allow the person who replaced me time to settle into the job and learn the ropes. I called Len Gullan and asked him if it would make any difference to him if I joined him at Admark later than we'd agreed.

He wasn't thrilled about my request but reluctantly agreed. "Okay John, I'll wait another five months. It will give you the chance to talk to your clients and perhaps you can encourage them to move their accounts over to Admark."

I left Muller & Phipps with my credibility intact. I'd worked especially hard over the last few months to ensure that the hand-over went smoothly. When I received my final salary cheque it occurred to me that they still owed me a considerable sum of money. I'd worked almost the whole of the previous year and yet they hadn't paid out my share of the profits or the bonus that I was entitled to. I decided to let it drop even though it was a chunk of my annual income but it taught me a salient lesson. Even some of the most respected companies either deliberately or by oversight fail to recognize the commitment of a valued employee when they move on.

On 1st December 1976 I stood at the threshold of a new career but unknown to me I was about to embark on a rollercoaster ride.

The first six months I spent with Admark were wonderful. It was a honeymoon period and I was doing what I loved most. I had gained a minor reputation at Muller & Phipps as a marketing guru and nothing gave me more of a buzz than pitching and winning new business. I enjoyed the warm and comforting feeling that whenever I secured new business it was not only for Admark's benefit but it would impact on my personal pocket.

I was basking in the glow of owning a share in a successful company.

During my notice period at Muller & Phipps I let our major clients know that I was joining Admark. Some were happy to move their advertising accounts to us because they wanted to take advantage of my marketing expertise and in-depth knowledge of their products and distribution patterns. It wasn't long before we had NCD, Ultramel, Elite and Tampax under our wing. This side of the business came so naturally to me but I still had to get to grips with my role as group managing director.

Len Gullan didn't bother me with the trivialities of the financial side of the business at first and it suited me fine since I had little more than a sketchy idea about debtors, creditors and cash flow. I was content to leave it to the expert.

The alarm bells only started ringing when I asked Gullan for an updated audited report. My lack of any formal financial training meant that I was hazy when it came to checking the statements and although the figures were more than a year old, to my untrained eye everything seemed fine and I was quite happy to pay for my 25% of the equity in the company based on the 1975 audited results.

In our initial meeting Gullan had vaguely made reference to an acquisition that he'd made sometime in 1976. The company he'd acquired was Greenwood Advertising and when I found out the details I was excited at the thought of owning an even bigger asset than I'd realized. In my imagination the rand signs were already multiplying and I could see that I'd soon be rich!

It didn't take long to find out that I knew absolutely nothing about finance. My ignorance of how to prepare budgets, analyze debtors and creditors or grasp the principles of cash flow or profit margins were soon exposed. This gulf in my education troubled me. How could I hope to run a group of companies, however small, without this kind of expertise?

When Gullan first approached me he was well aware of my reputation in the world of sales and marketing and had probably assumed that I also had sufficient financial acumen. I decided that I'd have to lean on the group financial director for a while. I was confident that he would lead me through the maze of figures. It wasn't long before I found out that he was utterly incompetent. It took rather more time to realize that he was crooked too.

Each time he asked me to countersign a cheque I noticed that it was always made out in round figures. I suggested to the financial director that it was quite a coincidence and I asked why there were never cheques made out for odd amounts but his explanation was evasive.

"You wouldn't understand John. We've got a bit of a cash squeeze on at the moment because some of our customers are a bit slow in paying. We stave off our creditors by paying them part of what we owe and it keeps them happy."

Was I being naïve to think that we shouldn't be incurring debts that we couldn't pay? I concluded that the financial director was not telling the truth. I was uneasy with his explanation because according to the last annual report the company was in a good position. I asked him for detailed trading figures since the last audited report and spent many hours laboriously ploughing through them. A nagging doubt about what had been going on without my knowledge overtook me. I concluded that not only had the financial director been spinning a web of lies but the administration was in a shambles and the finances were in dire straights.

This distressing state of affairs caused me many sleepless nights and I began to worry what I'd got myself into. I decided to go to the office on Saturdays when it was quiet and spend some time investigating a little more deeply. My worst fears were realized when I uncovered trays of unopened envelopes containing cheques from clients. Suppliers were banging on the door for payment and debtors and creditors hadn't been reconciled for months.

Nobody had the faintest idea what Admark's true trading position was or how much we owed our creditors. I may not have possessed any financial know-how but even a fool could see that we were in deep trouble. How deep was still unclear.

I collared our financial director and demanded answers from him. "Cut out your lame excuses and give it to me straight. It's obvious that we are in trouble but now I am asking you to tell the truth for a change and not a pack of lies."

He continued to shadow-box and trotted out a string of excuses and blamed staff changes and a breakdown of systems. It was at this juncture that it dawned on me that the position was ten times worse that I'd guessed. I was livid and couldn't wait to let Len Gullan know what I'd discovered. He expressed mild surprise but he fobbed me off with a vague wave of his hand, "You worry too much John. We'll put the system right and we'll be up and running in no time."

I was irritated because I expected Gullan to be concerned. Creditors were lining up for payment and yet we were still signing cheques for tiny amounts. None of it made sense. I took the bull by the horns and I decided that if Gullan wasn't interested I'd establish the company's exact trading position by systematically going through the debtors and creditors. Hopefully by doing that I could bring some order to the chaos.

I immediately got rid of the financial director and brought in Peter Baikie, the accountant from Muller & Phipps. I didn't want to recruit him under false pretences so I laid out the facts about the state of the company and sketched the worst-case scenario.

"Let's just say that the financial systems are non-existent. The books haven't been written up for months and we owe money all over town. We haven't a clue what our liabilities are. Do you still want the job?"

I waited for Peter to turn me down flat but he said that he'd give it his best shot. I was elated because although he wasn't a ball of fire I knew that he was a safe pair of hands. He wouldn't baulk at getting his hands dirty and more importantly he was honest, conscientious and ethical. In short he had all the qualities that his predecessor lacked. He understood that if he managed to steady things and get the company back on track that his move would be vindicated. He'd be earning a bigger salary and he'd have the status of director.

He buckled down and attacked the problem vigorously, but it was a long and tedious process. We worked together most weekends in an attempt to reconcile invoices with payments. We analyzed every scrap of data and wrote up the ledgers until we finally had a true picture of the company finances.

By mid-June in 1977 it was obvious to me that things were critical. Our liabilities exceeded our assets by more than R300 000 and the spectre of liquidation loomed. It was crystal clear why the company was sinking. The finger pointed straight at Len Gullan's door. It was his ill-conceived purchase of Greenwood Advertising that was dragging us down.

The wool had been pulled over his eyes when he bought Greenwood Advertising. In his eagerness to conclude the deal he hadn't waited for the audit to be finalized and went ahead with merging Admark with Greenwood. He'd assumed that the small positive asset shown in the previous year's Greenwood balance sheet would be much the same the following year. He went ahead in typical cavalier style and ended up with egg on his face. Without any real thought about the consequences Gullan took on all the Greenwood staff and merged the two companies at Admark even though he had not got rid of the lease on their premises. By the time it emerged that Greenwood had run at a huge loss over the last twelve months, it was too late.

Gullan had an ego the size of a battleship and he refused to acknowledge his blunder. He had committed a cardinal sin by failing to conduct a due diligence audit and we were left saddled with the Greenwood deal. We couldn't extricate ourselves from the mess and so we had to accept it as a fact of life and carry the massive liability that went with it. We were left with two options—to go under or somehow to trade our way out of the predicament that Gullan had landed us in.

I couldn't figure out why Gullan had done such a disastrous deal with Greenwood because whenever I watched him in meetings he seemed to be an extremely tough and uncompromising negotiator even to the extent of being economical with the truth. However for all his faults I had to admit that he always came across as intelligent, articulate and suave. In common with many dishonest people with whom I have had the misfortune to cross swords he unfailingly retained a calm unruffled manner and he seemed to be supremely self-confident.

Gullan first made his mark as a likeable and creative client service manager in the advertising field and then went on to establish a relatively successful direct response company. He'd managed to pick up his financial expertise somewhere along the way but in spite of his lack of formal qualification he set himself up as a pundit and was frequently called upon by radio stations to host money advice programmes. Whenever the annual budget was announced he would go to some studio, put the headphones on and give his own spin on events. He'd ask editors of financial publications probing questions on air and respond in such a way that everyone believed that he was the ultimate authority.

Though I'd slowly built up a picture of the company there was still a missing piece of the puzzle. I couldn't work out the arrangement that Len seemed to have with one of our international clients. I located sheaths of invoices made out to them but I couldn't trace a single payment. Every month I noticed that a credit had been passed and each new monthly statement reflected a nil balance. I asked Gullan why.

"The company has been remitting the outstanding amounts to an account in England. It's all legal and above board."

When I got to the bottom of this particular bit of financial juggling it was the final straw. Not only was the British bank account in the name of Len Gullan but he was acting in direct contravention of foreign exchange regulations by failing to repatriate the funds. He pointed out that he owned 100% of the company before he sold equity to me and as such it was his decision where he would leave any profit.

The discovery of these financial irregularities made my position untenable and I knew that unless I took immediate and drastic action I was going down the tubes. I was already pretty certain in my own mind that I had uncovered a massive fraud. I agonized over what I should do next. Calling the police in to investigate wasn't an option. I stood to lose everything and the thought of that made me break into a cold sweat. I would lose the house that I'd worked so hard to buy. It had cost R48 000 and I dreaded the idea of losing it.

My bargaining position was weak, after all I only owned 25% of the equity and Gullan held the rest. Apart from anything else, I knew that there was no going back. My career seemed to be in tatters particularly since I'd burned my bridges with Muller & Phipps. For a brief moment I thought of baling out but I knew that I was liable for a share of the company debt. It would have been impossible to return cap in hand to my old employers and it was likely no opposition company would have employed me as I was vastly over-qualified for a sales position.

I decided that the only course of action, however daunting, was to approach Gullan and offer to buy him out. He had deliberately deceived me and he had lied by omission about the financial state of the company. By this stage I had developed an ulcer and I spent many sleepless nights pacing my lounge hoping for some miracle escape route. In my experience this rarely happens and in testing times you must keep a cool head. I girded my loins and prepared to confront him.

I eventually pinned him down and said my piece. "Len, the finances of the company are in disarray, money has been siphoned off and you can't or won't explain it. I'm pretty sure that I know what you've been up to but I can't prove it. The truth of the matter is that I can't work with you and so I want to buy your share of the company. You can go your way and let me pick up the pieces."

I sat back and waited for the news to sink in and I was mildly surprised at his response.

"It suits me fine, John. If you think you've got enough to buy my 75% good luck. We'll sort out the numbers and you can carry on."

I'd already held several discussions with Barry Geere, the managing director of the advertising company and I had sounded him out about the possibility of getting rid of Gullan. Barry was solid and capable—a dyed in the wool advertising man. He'd been with the organization for many years and I suggested that if we could wrest the company from Gullan we could become equal partners. We agreed that if we could cut back on overheads and save Gullan's costs we had the chance to turn the business round and we could eventually wipe off the debt. We'd already approached the bank and they'd agreed in principle to lend us the money to buy Gullan's stake. I looked Gullan in the eye and said evenly, "You are asking far too much considering that the company is virtually on the rocks but I've organized the finance so we can do a deal right now."

"Good luck. I'm out, so take this as my resignation." Hours later he was gone. Within forty-eight hours of the deal being consummated I received a phone call from Gullan. His voice was flat and cold and I shuddered in anticipation of what he was about to tell me. I had no idea what a body blow he was about to deliver.

"I will destroy you personally and I will send Admark into oblivion."

The news was delivered in a measured and calculated tone and although I had little idea of what he meant by those chilling words it took less than a week to find out.

A week later in a blaze of publicity we learned that Gullan had been appointed as managing director of the South African Gold Coin Exchange. He was now the boss of Admark's largest account and with a single stroke of his pen he cancelled our relationship. It almost sounded the death knell for Admark.

I called the owner of SA Gold Coin Exchange to ask him to see me and reconsider the decision to drop Admark but he refused to see me. He cut me short and said, "It's not my baby. If you want our business you'll have to speak to Len. It's out of my hands."

I finally managed to see Gullan and his attitude was ruthless and cynical. He knew that he held the upper hand and his response was predictable. "You asked for it. You put me in a corner and forced me to sell my shares to you. Now I'm calling the shots and I will sit back and watch you go under."

We had to take action and there was no point in wallowing in self-pity. Cash flow was our greatest worry and we couldn't continue holding our creditors at bay by sending them part payment. We were bumbling along by only paying those persistent enough to keep calling for money.

I established how much we owed each of our creditors and then personally phoned them all to invite them to a creditors' meeting at our Twist Street office. Our premises were modest by any standards but we had the advantage of a low rent and abundant parking.

As I stood in front of the creditors I felt sick in the pit of my stomach. I'd never felt so nervous in my life and I sensed that the next half hour would be critical to our survival.

I began, "Ladies and gentlemen, thank you for attending this meeting today. Many of you will be wondering why I have asked you to be here. I'm afraid that I don't have good news for you. I'll be brief. Admark is virtually bankrupt and our liabilities exceed our assets. The company is in a shocking state and we owe a great deal of money. After you have heard what I have to say it will be up to you all to decide what course of action you want to take. You have two clear choices. You can send us into liquidation in which case you'll probably only get a couple of cents in the rand. However, if you are patient and you are prepared to trust me I promise to pay you all back in full."

A murmur went round the boardroom. It came as a shock to many of the audience. "I'd like to explain how we plan to go about things if you decide to wait for payment. We are not going to differentiate between any of our creditors; everybody will be treated exactly the same. We won't bow to pressure to pay more quickly than we can. Right now I'll give you my personal guarantee that every single cent of our profits will be used to pay off our debts and any new invoices that you present will be paid immediately."

I waited a moment before continuing, "Our books are open for you to check. You can see what and how much we owe. I will also give you details of our budget for the year ahead and what plans we have for any profit that we make. I promise that no member of our staff will get an increase and no director will get a bonus or dividend until all our debts are paid."

It was an impassioned plea and it was good to get things off my chest. I couldn't see any other way out as we needed to relieve the pressure on ourselves.

"In conclusion we need to concentrate on turning our business around and the last thing we need is to expend all our time and energy involved in crisis managment."

I could immediately sense that the mood of the meeting was positive. There seemed to be general understanding and approval of the way we intended to repay our debts. Our creditors unanimously accepted our proposal and we could breathe again.

It was a particularly distressing time for me because I hated having to publicly accept responsibility for the financial morass that we found ourselves in. During the next year we poured our energy into the business and tightened our belts wherever we could. We learned financial discipline and we rigorously followed the principle of 'a rand saved is a rand earned'. I emerged from financial virginity to become competent in reading balance sheets and mastering the intricacies of cash-flow charts.

At first it was tough to turn the ship but as time went on we began to make real progress. It finally took over four years to pay every one of our creditors in full. As a result we strengthened our relationship with them and in doing so it taught me to value the loyalty of our suppliers. It was an object lesson of how an honest, open and transparent approach pays dividends every time. Gullan refused to face reality, he didn't take remedial and he demonstrated an arrogant and callous approach to the very people that he should have nurtured.

Adcorp

Chapter 17

Birth of a giant

With Gullan consigned to history and the business beginning to come back on a firm footing it dawned on me that advertising wasn't as fulfilling as I'd imagined. The financial woes that I'd inherited had served to take my eye off the ball for a while but as the position eased I had more time to contemplate my future. It came as a wake-up call to find out that I didn't really like what I was doing.

Perhaps if I'd not spent a harrowing couple of years baling out the company it would have been different. On the other hand because I'd experienced a steep financial learning curve I understood the market much better. I realized that advertising was a segmented market and wasn't something that one could generalize about.

Because companies such as Coca-Cola, Ford Motor Company and Kellogg's spend billions to advertise their brand across the world, international brands are by far the most lucrative. These multi-national companies only appoint advertising agencies that have representative offices in all the world's major cities. McCann's for example handled Coca-Cola's account throughout the world. Admark wasn't internationally connected and so we couldn't pitch for the really big business.

A vast swathe of the local market was dominated by the Afrikaans-speaking community. Admark was most definitely an English-speaking agency and as such was excluded from pitching for business in organizations such as Sanlam or many of the large mining houses. The opportunity to bid for government business or parastatals was out of the question.

Admark was operating within a very narrow band. The competition was fierce and English-speaking companies changed their advertising agencies more frequently than their shirts. We'd lose major accounts on a whim, often because of factors beyond our control. A new marketing director would move into a company that we'd been doing business with and he'd immediately ditch us and shift his allegiance to an agency that he'd dealt with in his previous job. It irked me when we lost business like that and I felt uncomfortable doing business in such a small and volatile sector of the market. Bearing all these undeniable factors in mind we took the decision to sell Admark Advertising and look for opportunities elsewhere.

When I joined the company there was a very small division operating under the name Admark Recruitment Advertising that specialized in the design and placement of advertisements to recruit staff for major corporations. The recruitment advertising industry was in its embryonic stage and I could see a massive future for this type of business.

In a nutshell the business worked like this: Clients would consult with us after which we would identify their recruitment needs. From then on we'd create the advertisements, do the copy-writing, prepare the material for publication, and place the advertisement. Our expertise enabled us to select the most cost-effective media and those newspapers that would elicit the greatest response. Our clients didn't have to pay for this service as we derived our revenue from the media in the form of commission. I was enthusiastic about the potential of the business. As it turned out Admark Recruitment was the first block in the matrix that ultimately became Adcorp.

When we decided to direct our energies into Admark Recruitment Advertising our first task was to position it correctly. This was where I felt at home. I set about analyzing our target market and where we'd get the best response.

I decided to play to our strengths and put the Afrikaans segment of the market on hold. We attacked the largest and most powerful organizations in the English-language segment of the commercial and industrial market. We successfully captured business from Anglo American, De Beers and Woolworths and most of the other blue chip companies in the country. It speaks volumes for the professionalism of our staff and quality of management that thirty years later they have retained these mega accounts.

Our growth was phenomenal and in May of our first year we turned over R50 000. Twelve months later in May we doubled our business and then repeated the feat the following year. It exceeded my wildest dreams because I knew that we were ploughing a fertile field nobody had tilled before.

Kellogg's were the masters of the divide-and-rule philosophy. I'd learned this strategy at Muller & Phipps when I handled their account. Kellogg's dominated the breakfast cereal market and they ensured that by going into competition with themselves they wouldn't be knocked off their perch. They understood that when you are successful with a product it won't be long before a competitor arrives on the scene. Kellogg's were highly successful in manufacturing and marketing cornflakes but they were smart enough to know that before an opposition company could beat them to the punch and grab a share of their market, it would be critical for them to launch new cereal brands.

Kellogg's systematically swamped the market by manufacturing Sugar Pops, Rice Krispies, Honey Smacks, Raisin Bran and a host of other cereal brands. They spent vast sums on research and they countered any competitor's move by switching their advertising thrust to go head to head with any new similar product that threatened their brand. They achieved their objective by price-cutting and by increasing their advertising and marketing budget. The strategy made them into a winning company and they became the model for every Admark operation.

I appointed Robin Clive to run Admark because of his remarkable talent. His efforts contributed enormously to our rapid expansion. I discovered later that he was something of a Walter Mitty character and it puzzled me because he had no need to tell tall stories about his achievements. Clients liked to be in his company so I never understood why he felt compelled to portray himself as something he wasn't. He obviously harboured an inferiority complex but I didn't know why.

His stories were told with such a straight face that I think that he actually believed the tales himself! The trouble was that he never remembered who he'd told his ridiculous and wildly imaginative stories to and at times when he repeated himself the stories became more elaborate.

He once told a group of our business associates that he'd been secretly seconded to the Israelis during the Six Day War. We all had a fair idea how old he was and by a process of simple arithmetic we concluded that he was fourteen at the time he was commanding a tank squadron deep inside Sinai!

I'd heard some of his more outrageous anecdotes many times but one particular story about his rugby exploits was downright embarrassing. We were invited to join one of our business associates for a big game at Ellis Park. Something happened in the far corner of the ground after a scrum and the referee whistled up for an offence that none of us understood. Robin jumped in and went into a rambling technical explanation of what had happened. A chap sitting next to him said, "I'm impressed Robin. I didn't know that you knew the game so well."

Robin said, "Well, you probably don't know that I played top rugby in my time."

This invited the question: "Sorry, I didn't know. Who did you play for?"

Without missing a beat he replied, "Well, my most memorable game was when I played for the Barbarians against the Springboks at Twickenham."

I never heard anything so absurd and I could have crawled under the seat. To my surprise our hosts took his story as gospel. Why not? From that day on they treated him with respect and never for one moment did anyone doubt his preposterous line of bull.

I'd played squash with Robin a few times and he was a complete rabbit. I was no great shakes but I could see that he was totally bereft of any kind of hand-eye coordination. I'd have staked my life that he never made it beyond his prep school fifth side!

We often used to have lunch at a marvellous restaurant named St Germain. It was just downstairs from our Joubert Park offices and the owner was Germain Maquis who created food to die for. He was a flamboyant Frenchman and his streak of individuality endeared him to his regular patrons. Robin was the exception. Germain couldn't get his name right and he constantly referred to him as Clive. It drove Robin mad but he never found out if Germain was just sending him up.

When Robin decided to return to England in 1979 he was succeeded by Paul Hutchins. Paul did sterling service for Admark for many years and he was a delight to have around. His intelligence and sense of humour made him a prized asset.

Tragedy struck Paul soon after he joined the company and it changed his life forever. One evening after working late at the office his car was involved in a horrendous accident with a Putco bus. He was rushed to a hospital in Pretoria but in spite of receiving specialist attention he was left paralyzed from the waist down.

His friends supported him through tough times and there were always visitors at his bedside to lift his spirits and help him through his depression. I often went to see Paul with Germain who used to smuggle in delicious meals right under the noses of curious nursing staff.

Once a week he'd get a visit from the van Rensburg ladies. They were three sisters who all worked at Admark, but as far as Paul was concerned they were angels of mercy. Without fail, once a week, they'd be there to give Paul a total makeover. They'd cut and buff his nails, shampoo his hair and massage him with oil and he often told me that when he was in the depths of despair he cherished those moments.

I hardly knew what to say when I first went to see Paul in hospital. One day he was a virile, lively personality and the next time I saw him he was a mere shell of a man unable to move and lying on his back in unspeakable pain. What does one say in such times? No words are adequate to reassure a man whose life has been destroyed in a second.

I assured him that his position would remain open for however long it took him to recover. As things turned out his rehabilitation was a long and tortuous road but he made it back—albeit in a wheelchair.

His courage and cheerful demeanour was an inspiration to everyone. Even when he was suffering he never complained and he remained positive. He even joked about his disability and one day he called into the office to say that the tyre on his wheelchair was punctured and he was stuck in traffic and couldn't make it in to work!

I owe him a personal debt of gratitude for his unstinting effort to drive the company forward and in spite of his handicap he never allowed it to hamper his work. He set a remarkable example to us all of how to turn adversity into triumph.

So, first with Robin and then for a much longer period with Paul, we built Admark Recruitment Advertising into the most successful business in its field. My next task was to investigate other avenues that would allow me to build on that success.

Chapter 18

New horizons

I certainly never claimed to be hands-on in the recruitment business. My role was to see the big picture and chart the way forward. My days were spent exploring growth and development opportunities.

I was determined to expand operations to Cape Town and Durban and I soon identified possible targets. I was close to setting up companies in both centres when I received a surprise call.

Altolevel, a smaller company than Admark in Johannesburg, had opened and dominated the recruitment advertising market in both Cape Town and Durban. Their success was largely due to the sterling efforts of Val Middleton and Caroline Bishop who were the driving forces behind the business. They asked for a meeting with me to discuss their future. When they called all I knew was that they intended to leave Altolevel—apart from that I was in the dark!

When we met it soon became apparent that they had come to see me because they both wanted to join Adcorp. Their timing couldn't have been better but I was mystified as to why they would resign from an organization that was doing so well.

When I quizzed them, the answer was not at all what I expected. Val acted as the spokesman. "We are frustrated and fed up with empty promises. We were told that if we performed well we'd be given shares in the company and that we'd both be appointed as directors. It's just been hot air. We've given our best but still nothing has happened."

I could see a gap big enough to drive a bus through and I jumped at the opportunity to get these dynamic women on board. Neither was tied by any restraint agreements and they didn't have any kind of restrictive notice period.

"It will take me a while to iron out the details but I would love you to be part of Admark because it would open the door for us to become a national company. I'll structure a deal that will give you the directorships you want and you'll get equity in your own companies."

They were thrilled at the prospect and I was elated at the thought of having offices in Cape Town and Durban. In the process Admark would significantly increase its market share.

Armed with their agreements Val and Caroline resigned from Altolevel and then called their staff together to inform them of their decision. Admark had to tread carefully because we didn't want to be accused of poaching the Altolevel staff, but within days all of them had approached me for a job. In the service industry, charismatic leaders develop a nucleus of personal clients who will follow them regardless of what company they work for. With Val and Caroline gone, the support staff realized that their jobs would have been vulnerable.

Overnight Admark had a viable business and a sound client base in Durban and Cape Town. We doubled in size and immediately created an organization five times greater than our nearest competitor.

Once the companies were fully integrated, running smoothly and showing good profits my thoughts turned to other ways to grow the business. We had the English-language segment tied up and the next logical step was to find the key that would unlock the lucrative Afrikaans sector.

Blue-chip English-speaking companies were primarily located in Johannesburg whereas the Afrikaans market was largely based in Cape Town. The remedy was to create a new company in which every employee spoke Afrikaans as a first language. I knew that this was the key to breaking into companies such as Sanlam, Old Mutual and Rembrandt. I established

Effective Recruitment Advertising and installed a top professional named Zuretha Olivier to run the show and in no time we won new business from all the big companies.

We soon became victims of our own success and because of our total dominance the market began to fragment. This development meant one thing. It was time to implement 'The Kellogg's Strategy'.

If I created our own competition I could establish the rules of the game. The hunt was on for further acquisitions that would give us organic growth while being strategically relevant.

My analogy whenever I was asked to explain my philosophy was, "Our organic growth will help us to climb the stairs, but acquisitions will allow us to take the elevator to the top floor."

Chapter 19

Fitting it all together

You don't pick up bargain buys in the service industry. I feel very strongly about this.

High-quality, well-trained and motivated people make the wheels go round in top companies. If you want the best you must be prepared to pay a premium. I never wavered in my determination to acquire companies that were leaders in their field.

When I tried to acquire a new company my negotiations were never driven by the desire to knock down the asking price. It is a golden rule that unless the personnel that contribute to the success of a company stay with the organization there is no point in buying it.

Because we never compromised on quality staff it was invariably necessary for us to charge more for our services. This sounds great in principle but cost-conscious clients are often unwilling or unable to differentiate between good and bad service. The consequence of this is that they are frequently unwilling to pay a premium. The more I encountered resistance to price the more I worried that we could become vulnerable.

I approached Paul Brand who was the owner and managing director of Altolevel, who had formed the company's Cape Town and Durban operations that had now broken away to join Adcorp. I had always admired Paul's professional ability and I knew that he commanded his clients' loyalty. What I also liked about him was that people tagged him as a maverick and the fact that he didn't toe the corporate line. I convinced him to sell his company and join the Admark group.

Altolevel was an excellent company and we had frequently banged heads with them in Johannesburg. I knew that once we had them in our stable I could relax if there was a price war in the industry. I planned to use Altolevel as a buffer between Admark Recruitment (by far the largest agency) and any up and coming rival company. It gave me peace of mind to know that Paul was waiting in the wings if Admark was attacked on price but as it happened the price war was a non-event and any threat soon fizzled out.

In bringing in Altolevel, we achieved our first objective and that was to increase our market penetration. I developed a strategy that would eventually see us commanding the entire recruitment advertising market. Our group of agencies at this point held about 55% of the total market share and our eight or so competitors held the balance.

Some of the principles that had become second nature to me at Muller & Phipps were not being applied to the recruitment advertising business and I couldn't see why not.

In the supermarket world heavy hitters like Checkers, Pick 'n Pay and OK Bazaars squeezed the suppliers for lower prices. They rightly reasoned that if they bought more of a particular product than a small concern they should pay less. They used their muscle and it made them successful.

I asked myself why the same thing shouldn't apply to the advertising industry and it bugged me. Deep down I knew that I needed to address the issue and work toward changing the way newspapers were doing business with their biggest customers.

I set up a meeting with Chris Booysen who I knew socially. He was the marketing chief at the *Sunday Times* and over the years we have remained firm friends. He was sympathetic but explained that any major shift in policy would need the approval of Stephen Mulholland.

Stephen, the managing director, was an internationally respected businessman who famously saved the *Sunday Times* from the brink of bankruptcy. He successfully turned an ailing giant into a profitable

Top: John with his parents in Alexandria, Egypt, aged 6.
Above: John, aged 16, ready for his first day at work at the bank.
Right: The Koo-ee, John's tearoom, West Street, Durban. Business acquired at age 18.

Top: Entrance to St Joseph's College, Darjeeling, India.
Above: St Joseph's College in the foreground with the ice-capped peaks of the Himalayan Mountains as the backdrop.

juggernaut. I knew in my heart that he'd be a tough nut to crack.

Each week I received a detailed analysis of the total number of column centimetres our advertising agencies placed with the *Sunday Times* compared to how many were placed by each of our key competitors. We were taking more and more advertising space while our opposition were falling back; their business with the *Sunday Times* was either static or declining.

It is the advertising that makes any newspaper profitable and without it they would barely cover their costs. In the case of the *Sunday Times*, recruitment advertising was particularly profitable and enough to warrant a fairly substantial supplement that frequently contained forty pages.

When I met Stephen Mulholland I was well prepared and I had my facts and figures at my finger tips.

"Chris and I discussed the matter of an increased discount for companies a few weeks ago. The *Sunday Times* makes a lot of money out of the recruitment supplement and we are by far and away your biggest advertiser. Now that you have all the data you can see just how much we are spending compared with everybody else. I'd like you to consider giving us a more generous rebate than we are receiving at present."

After a tough bout of bargaining Stephen finally conceded that our business did indeed warrant a better deal. His agreement represented a major coup for us. A well-managed recruitment advertising agency generally managed to show pre-tax profits that were twice as high as those of a conventional advertising agency. Both types of business received 16.5% commission but in our case our expenses were far lower.

Image counts for a great deal in the glitzy world of advertising. To maintain such sumptuous surroundings these agencies have to pay exorbitantly high rentals which serve to place a huge burden on their overheads. Salaries too are a major expense and if any agency wants to entice the top creative directors and media executives they have to pay top dollar.

Recruitment advertising, however, is far from being a high-flying industry. Our clients rarely visited the company offices and our business didn't rely on highly creative people or fat-salaried media specialists. We were free to work from more downbeat offices and as a result we could contain our overheads. Recruitment advertising didn't rely on TV, radio, billboards or magazines—every single cent we spent was with the newspapers.

We managed to operate at a pre-tax profit of 6% of turnover, as opposed to conventional agencies that were lucky to scrape by on an average of 3%. All things considered, our margins were very acceptable bearing in mind that our gross earnings were only 16.5%.

The extra rebate that I managed to extract from the *Sunday Times* went straight to our bottom line and that was the beauty of the deal. A mere 3% more discount from them had the instant effect of increasing our margin to 9% and in doing so increased our profitability by 50%. When these discounts were added to the savings that we were making on our tightly controlled administration systems and healthy cash flows, our margins were something that conventional agencies could only dream of.

Chapter 20

Getting burned offshore

For the first four years after Barry Geere and I took over at Admark we struggled to clear off our debts. We began to make operating profits but true to our promise to our creditors, not a cent went into our pockets.

Our move into the recruitment advertising business was perfectly timed. We started when it was in its infancy but a few years later in 1980 there was a dramatic upswing. South African industry and commerce was brimming with optimism and there was runaway growth. Suddenly there was an acute shortage of skills.

Top businesses turned to us, as the largest recruitment advertising group in South Africa, to help them fill their many vacancies. South Africa was an attractive country to work in—housing was cheap and the weather was good. We had no trouble in attracting skilled people from Europe to settle in the land of 'Blue skies, braaivleis and Chevrolets'. In no time at all we became the major conduit for overseas skilled people.

South Africa's apparently insatiable hunger for skilled people led to us spending heavily on recruitment advertisements in the international media. We placed our newspaper advertisements through local agents who took a disproportionately high 10% commission for very little effort while we were left with 5%.

Despite disagreeing with the government of the time, I had immense faith in South Africa's future and I couldn't visualize the flood of skilled people to the country ever drying up. Consequesntly, I saw no earthly reason why we couldn't save the huge amounts of commission we were giving away if we started our own operation in England. So in 1980 I travelled to London to open a recruitment advertising agency.

My motives for opening up for business in England were not wholly confined to preserving additional commission. I'd examined how the British approached recruitment advertising and it appeared to me that we operated far more professionally in South Africa. I figured that we could crack the market open if we could find a way of replicating the way we did business back home.

For many years we'd been experiencing an acute shortage of skilled people in South Africa and the demand always exceeded the supply of high-calibre employees. To succeed in the recruitment business in South Africa you had to sharpen your wits and work harder and smarter otherwise you would fall by the wayside.

In England the converse was true and to fill employment vacancies it was just a matter of placing an advertisement in the 'Situations Vacant' column of the newspaper and sitting back. Without any effort, creativity or copywriting skills on the part of the agency, applications would just flood in.

Starting up a business was a massive frustration and I had no idea that I'd have to clear so many obstacles before I could get going. In my mind I didn't anticipate any initial problems and I expected it would be a breeze. I'd been led to believe that the British were super-efficient and we South African businessmen tended to have the impression that they were far ahead of us.

I had my first brush with British bureaucracy when I tried to open a bank account. My hands were tied and I wasn't able to sign office leases or buy equipment until I had one.

In my innocence I thought that after arranging to meet the bank manager at nine o'clock on Monday morning, he would actually keep the appointment! I arrived at the bank bang on time and announced myself. I was surprised when the receptionist smiled sweetly and said, "Oh yes,

Mr Barry. I see that you are expected, but the manager only gets to the office at ten!"

While I sat idly around paging through magazines, people gradually began trickling into the reception area. I was becoming exasperated and when the clock ticked past ten I couldn't contain my frustration any longer. I approached the secretary, "Excuse me but I've come all the way from Johannesburg and I don't have much time. I've got several appointments this morning. Can you tell me how long the manager will be?"

"I'm sorry Mr Barry, but he has just arrived and there are two people ahead of you."

I was highly irritated and demanded that she went to the manager to explain that I had to see him at once. She obviously sensed my growing agitation and finally common sense prevailed and I got my interview. A few days in London were enough for me to find out that the more senior you were in an organization the shorter the hours you were expected to work! Unlike the culture back home where management tended to work long hours, English executives arrived later and left earlier than their underlings!

Over the next few years I used to fly to England every couple of months to monitor the growth of the operation. I learned fairly quickly how difficult it is to manage a company at arm's length. I became disillusioned by the staff's couldn't-care-less attitude toward work. None of them mirrored the philosophy, commitment and enthusiasm of the Admark employees back home. I tried extremely hard to engender these work ethics in London but it proved an elusive dream. We increased turnover and built the business, but there was a spark missing.

I was approached by Mike, a talented recruitment specialist who had become disenchanted by the way he'd been treated by his employer. He was aggrieved because he'd been given short shrift by his company and wanted to join an organization that would give him a share of the equity. I saw huge potential and so we agreed terms and established a new company to focus on recruiting local staff for local companies.

Just as the business was starting to move in the right direction and I was allowing myself to become optimistic about our progress, in 1983, a sudden backlash from the trade unions rocked us onto our heels.

It came like a bolt of lightning. Without warning or any kind of negotiation, a representative of the type-setters' union informed the national UK newspapers that its members would strike if they accepted another advertisement from us. They'd got wind of a South African connection. It was the kind of irrational apartheid backlash that we'd dreaded so much and it finally led to the media delivering a blow to the solar plexus!

It was a near-fatal punch and one that had us on the ropes. I was devastated. We were rendered impotent and were forced to close. We had every justification for declaring ourselves insolvent but once again we bit the bullet, paid our creditors from South African funds and baled out.

Shortly after we closed our British operations Barry Geere decided that he wanted to explore another avenue of business. We had been operating successfully for six years and I wanted to expand even further so we agreed to go our own ways and there were no hard feelings. I offered to buy Barry's shares in the company and he was happy. I agreed to his asking price for his 50% share and in doing so I became the sole owner of Admark.

Barry and I had been more than business partners; we were close friends and the parting was sad. I plunged myself deep into debt but I didn't stress about the bank loan because the potential was limitless and my ambition was to bring my vision and dreams to fruition.

Chapter 21

Leading from the front

By 1985 Admark had grown large enough for me to make some basic strategic changes. I felt that it was time to impose some of my strategic ideas across the spectrum.

More than anything else I wanted every Admark company to have a CEO that would lead by personal example. It was my aim to cultivate an army of fighters, a calibre of professional sales people that were prepared to stick their chins out. I vowed to encourage my top executives to go to war, break down doors, get their hands dirty and embrace the cut and thrust of pitching for new accounts.

I identified certain highly motivated people that surrounded themselves with a loyal following of clients. These sales people were the kind of dynamic individuals who recognized how valuable their clients were to their business and were prepared to go to the ends of the world for them. I recognized that the downside of encouraging my people to make this fierce commitment to their clients would be that administrative discipline would probably fly out the window. These were people prepared to go into the fire but they wouldn't necessarily always pick up the debris.

I had watched at first hand how Len Gullan's demise had been caused by his spectacular failure to address the administrative details. He certainly wasn't the first super-salesman to push the self-destruct button. I had to avoid it happening to us.

In my experience sales and marketing people tend to close their eyes and pretend that debtors, creditors, profits, losses and ratios don't concern them. They are driven forward by a vision of rising turnover and spiralling billing figures and they treat financial discipline as a mere irritation. It is this thrusting mentality that motivates good sales people but, unfortunately, eventually they have to wake up. They come to realize that like mother doing their laundry—it doesn't last forever!

My basic management philosophy is to let people play to their greatest strengths. Our business was propelled by dynamic marketing and sales people. I wanted them to be out in the field doing what they did best. I wanted them to capture new business, mentor new sales trainees and keep our clients happy. Invariably it was at the expense of administration so I took care of the problem by lifting the responsibility from their shoulders. I centralized all accounting and administration procedures of all our operations in our Johannesburg HQ.

I set our staff free from the onerous accounts work that they detested so much. With the new measures in place none of them needed to raise an invoice, order goods, worry about debtors or creditors, enter into a lease, or pay for anything. I established an independent, centralized accounts and administration office that had the immediate effect of slashing our expenses and increasing our profits. More importantly our key people were released to chase new business and cultivate client relationships.

I could no longer tear myself into a thousand pieces. We had grown quickly and too many people were demanding a few moments of my time each day and I was not able to focus on expanding the business. It was a tough choice that I had to make, but I opted to divest myself of the day to day decision-making and return to my roots.

I often draw the comparison between company managing directors and army generals. Some sit high on a hill and command their officers while viewing the battle from a distance. Others lead their troops into battle. I have always preferred the latter type of general and so I spent my days foraging for new business, searching for potential acquisitions and keeping my eyes open for growth opportunities.

I still got a big buzz from calling on our clients personally. I always took an Admark sales executive with me and it was a perfect chance for me to monitor their progress and fine-tune their selling skills. I could guide them through delicate negotiations while they in turn could absorb the knowledge to pass it on to up-and-coming sales people. It was pleasing to find out how flattered and appreciative our clients were to see me because that kind of personal touch was becoming rare in business and my presence served to assure them of how much we valued their support.

I knew that the danger existed that I might neglect the company's financial affairs and that I would need to delegate some of my responsibilities. That was when Tony Worthington came into my life.

I could feel an immediate affinity with him when we first met. I was impressed with his string of credentials and I offered him a newly created position as group financial director. Tony had trained as a chartered accountant and he'd left a glittering career with Barings Bank in London. It was there that he'd built up invaluable connections with the major banking houses and members of the stock exchange. From the day he joined Admark I stopped worrying about anything that was under his control and I trusted him implicitly. What began as a purely business association developed into an enduring friendship and ultimately a partnership. Tony's arrival left me free to create a vision and develop our strategy.

Tony became a close confidant and I used him as a valuable sounding board and listening post. Sometimes he underestimated the impact of his wisdom on my thinking. I remember him saying once, "You never seem to concentrate on anything I ever say."

I remember replying, "Tony, I always pay attention to everything that you say although I often don't do what you say. What you don't realize is how many times I have changed course because of your advice."

I constantly reminded myself that I had decided to get into business to create wealth and ultimately to unlock that wealth. My desire and ambition didn't change with the passing years. However, I had to remind myself that in building and developing any business, when it is time to sell it will only be worth what somebody else is prepared to pay for it.

Our profits were growing. We were spending massively with South Africa's newspapers and the increased discounts that we extracted from the *Sunday Times* made our bottom line look very healthy. We had such a grip on the recruitment advertising market that it was inevitable that that our rapid rate of growth would begin to slow. New opportunities were scarce and to avoid the risk of stagnation it was imperative for us to enter a new field.

With this in mind I realized that we should maximize the skills that we already possessed. Clearly it would make good sense to exploit our expertise in another area of the service industry. We had built an enviable client list and our ability to build on those close relationships was paramount. These criteria were in the forefront of my mind as I combed the market for new ventures in the intellectual property field.

I set myself a simple target. For me to consider buying any new business it was essential that it was already highly successful. It had to be absolutely top quality and furthermore not afraid to charge premium prices. I was convinced that customers will always recognize top quality and when they do, are prepared to pay a little more for it.

My aim was to identify quality companies. It has been my experience that if one enters an entirely new field it saves a great deal of effort, time and money if you make a sound acquisition. An existing company has a history, a philosophy and strategy and it is these elements that can provide the kick-start.

The real conundrum after setting out the ground rules was how we could make such an acquisition when we didn't have the funds?

Chapter 22

Listing on the JSE

I decided to explore the possibility of listing Admark on the Johannesburg Stock Exchange. My thoughts about raising capital through a listing on the stock exchange began as no more than a vague idea but the more I considered it a possibility, the more it excited me. It seemed fairly logical that unlocking the value of our business would help us realize the capital needed to spread our wings. At the time I had little concept of the obstacles or technicalities that lay ahead.

As I began to make initial investigations about how I could push the process forward I discovered that the red tape governing the rules and regulations on the JSE were daunting. Not least of all the hurdles, was the requirement for aspirants to produce a healthy balance sheet. On the face of it, ours was far from impressive.

I tried to get to grips with what criteria would be essential for me to take the next step. I gradually started to compile some sort of list of companies that had successfully launched themselves on the JSE main board. I thought that it would be helpful to know what they did, how they were rated and why. It would have been of immense help if there were a model for me to copy, but on closer examination I discovered that apart from the major financial institutions there was no other company that was listed that dealt in intellectual capital. If we went ahead it would mean breaking the mould.

When owners of private businesses decide to sell they are usually disappointed to find out that they are bargaining from a position of weakness and rarely get paid what they genuinely think is a fair reflection of the value. When they arrive at the point when they decide to sell there are usually two possible categories of purchasers—a partner or a competitor. Therein lies the root of the problem.

Partners are invariably cash-strapped after taking on huge bank loans to buy into the business in the first place. They are unlikely to be in a position to acquire any further equity. The alternative is to sit at the bargaining table with your competitors but that is not an attractive option as the price is driven down when they sense that you have no one else to talk to.

I reasoned that if I took Admark onto the JSE rather than try to sell the business outright I would be left with a tangible asset in the form of shares rather than a pile of cash. The value of the company would be reflected in the share price. Those shares could in turn be swapped for equity in other businesses.

Having made up my mind to pursue this avenue I needed a clear vision of what areas of the service industry would be compatible with the business I knew best. Throughout my career I had seen the value of detailed and comprehensive research and I knew there were no short cuts.

I had long and exhausting meetings with our clients with the sole aim of discovering what key services they used that made their lives easier. When I disseminated all the facts and figures I was able to narrow my search. I found that time and time again I'd been told that there was a pressing need for a market research and public relations company that would provide a genuinely pro-active service.

When I looked around there was no shortage of public relations companies but most of them appeared to do little more than react to their clients' instructions. Such organizations were ten-a-penny but I was not interested in them. I ruled them out. My concept of excellence was only to be found in those rare companies that reached out to their clients. I was interested in the ones that ensured that they were at the very heart of their clients' planning and implementation strategy and were not merely reactive to their needs.

I was quickly able to discard 90% of the companies in the PR arena that I surveyed. When that was done, I began the serious task of separating the wheat from the chaff. From that point on it was an easy selection process because one company stood out like a shining beacon.

That company was TWS and it fitted the bill perfectly. It was five times larger than its nearest rival and had offices in Johannesburg, Cape Town and Durban. It was, however, not only its size that I found appealing. TWS provided more than just a superficial, lightweight public relations package. They were immensely strong in financial strategizing and they had no equal in the field of communications. Their expertise extended far beyond pure public relations but it expanded into crisis management and media communications. They were also instrumental in assisting several of their clients through the tangled maze leading to stock exchange listing.

The detailed preparation and planning for our JSE listing involved us in a mountain of paper work. We enlisted the help of Tony Berman, the senior partner at Werksmans, to act as our attorney. Berman had the distinction of being the only South African lawyer to make the list of the world's top one hundred legal brains. I always felt comfortable talking to Tony because he had the remarkable gift of explaining complex legal issues in language that I could easily understand.

We were on the verge of tying up the loose ends for our JSE listing when Tony threw me a curved ball. He was completing a form that related to company directors.

"I assume that you are married."

I answered in the affirmative. Wendi, my second wife and I had got married in 1973.

"Married antenuptial contract," he intoned almost as a knee-jerk reaction. He seemed anxious to move quickly through the questions. My reply stopped him in mid-sentence.

"No," I said. "I'm actually married in community of property."

He stopped and looked at me aghast. "You're what?"

"I'm married in community of property," I repeated.

"I don't believe you! Why would any man in his right mind do that?" he asked. "I never thought about it when I got married. The last thing that entered my mind was tax or finances or anything like that."

"Well John," he said. "You're out of your mind. We have to change all that!"

"Please explain what the problem is. Why can't I just leave things as they are?"

He put his pen down, sighed, leaned back in his chair and ticked off reasons on his fingers in the way a mother might explain why her son can't stay up late to watch TV on a school day!

"John, you amaze me! Can you even begin to understand the implications if you die rich?"

"I've got that angle covered. When I die my life insurance policies will pay out and that will be more than enough to cover any estate duties."

"Ah, but have you got any idea what will happen if your wife dies first?"

I suddenly saw what he was driving at and it dawned on me that I hadn't been so smart after all.

"Gee, I never thought about it like that. Are you telling me that if Wendi doesn't have insurance policies the joint estate would be wound up? If that happened I'd have massive problems."

"Exactly! You'll have to do something about it. You'll have to change that. You can't be married in community of property. You have to get divorced."

"DIVORCED? Isn't there some other loophole?"

"No chance. The only way you can change the legal status of a relationship is by getting divorced. Then, assuming that you want to remarry, you will draw up a new antenuptial contract and you'll avoid any tax implications."

My head was in a spin. When I walked into his office I was happily married. Now I was agreeing to get divorced!

"Okay, if you think that's the best way for me, can you arrange to do the divorce for me?"

"I'm sorry John. That's out of the question. You've just told me that you are happily married. If I arrange your divorce I would perjure myself. You'll have to find another lawyer. If you tell him another story it's your choice."

I was flabbergasted, but I mulled over what he'd told me. A day later I was sitting in front of a very charming, high profile lawyer whom Tony Berman had recommended.

"Good morning. I want a divorce please!"

"I don't normally handle divorces but as Tony Berman has referred you to me I'll help you. Can you outline some of your reasons for wanting to take this drastic step?"

I hadn't given any thought to the issue. I thought that one walked in, asked for a divorce, signed a paper, paid a fee and that was it. I didn't expect him to ask what grounds my request was based on. I had to think on my feet. I blurted out the first thing that came into my head,

"Irreconcilable differences."

It sounded quite convincing and I was quite impressed with myself for having come up with such a glib answer. "Can you elaborate on these irreconcilable differences?"

I was afraid of opening a can of worms so I knew that I'd have to tread carefully. "It's rather personal. But why do you need to know the details? I'm told that people get divorced all the time for irreconcilable differences."

He said, "The court will ask. They don't grant divorces without a valid reason. You'll have to demonstrate that you have really tried to make up your differences."

I was deflated. The way Tony explained things it seemed to be a simple formality. The questions seemed to be getting out of hand so I called an end to the meeting and said that I'd like more time to think it over.

Our second meeting didn't go any better. He pressed me even harder for answers and I began to shadow-box. I was becoming confused and eventually I couldn't take his probing any longer.

"Look, I know what I told you before, but now I feel that I must confess to the real problem. It's actually all my fault and my wife is not at all to blame. I've been working long hours and I've neglected her. We argue all the time."

He gave me a piercing look that made me squirm in my chair. "I find it strange. The people I come across that ask me to arrange a divorce never have a good word to say about their spouse. They spend the whole time whingeing and moaning yet you go to extreme lengths to tell me how wonderful your wife is. You certainly are an honourable man. Why you want a divorce is beyond me."

I wanted the floor to open up and swallow me. He was complimenting me on what was a pack of lies. I desperately wanted to come clean but I was driven on by the fear that he would send me packing. I began to embellish my story until at last he stopped his questioning. I knew that he didn't believe me but he agreed to go ahead.

Wendi understood why we had to get divorced but it troubled her. One day her insecurity spilled over. "Perhaps after the divorce goes through you won't want to get married to me again!"

I felt awful inside and did everything I could to assure her. I even offered to cede half our assets. She was mollified but I could sense her unease.

My day in court was a real eye-opener for me as I'd never set foot in a magistrate's court before and the sheer drabness and hopelessness of the place depressed me. I hated the thought that I was about to go through a ridiculous charade that would see my marriage annulled.

Dozens of people were lined up on the benches waiting for their cases to be heard. There was an air of bitterness and acrimony pervading the mood of the plaintiffs. I listened to an endless litany of sordid cases. Couples aired their dirty laundry in front of the magistrate, but it barely took a couple of minutes for him to terminate their marriages. People appeared happy as they walked away—free at last from the bickering and fighting that had led them there in the first place.

My name was called and even though I knew my case was different, I was trembling for some strange reason. Perhaps the magistrate was bored by granting quickie divorces. He chose me of all people to probe for reasons, but after a short while he granted my request. I was all for rushing straight out and getting married all over again but my lawyer cautioned me not to lay myself open to perjury.

Nine months later I married Wendi for a second time. I can't say that all our friends completely understood the reason why, but they enjoyed a memorable black-tie evening at Les Marquis and for the one and only time Germain broke all his own rules and allowed a band into his hallowed restaurant!

At the time that Adcorp first listed on the JSE Tony Worthington and I were the only executive directors. It was a JSE requirement that there should be a minimum of four directors. I realized that it would be important to raise our profile and that we had to gain public credibility by inviting respected, high-achieving individuals to join our board.

John MacKenzie was a personal friend and he was extremely well connected. He had an engineering background and had recently retired as general manager of CDM as well as serving on the Anglo American board. I knew him as a man of outstanding intellect and integrity and when he accepted my invitation to join the Adcorp board I was delighted. Over the years he contributed immensely and was always extremely well prepared for meetings and possessed a rare quality of grasping the details of any subject tackled.

My next task was to bring equilibrium to the board as the perception was that we were far too 'English'. I needed to redress this imbalance and to this end I set about finding a highly regarded individual from the Afrikaans community. Looking back I wonder how I had the temerity to write to Dr Francois Jacobsz to ask him to consider joining the Adcorp board. After all we were a relatively small JSE company engaged in the intellectual capital business. Dr Jacobsz was an industrial giant and a political heavyweight. He headed Union Steel in Vereeniging and his legal advisor at one time was FW de Klerk. In fact it was FW de Klerk who persuaded Dr Jacobsz to enter politics. He went on to become the first National Party candidate to win a seat from the PFP. Later he was appointed as chairman of the Parliamentary Finance committee.

It was much to my surprise that Dr Jacobsz responded positively to my letter and agreed to meet me for lunch to discuss my proposal. After I outlined the details of the company and I expressed my vision for Adcorp he agreed to join our board. He told me that he was excited at the prospect of becoming involved in a service industry company as he had been an industrialist all his business life.

It was the beginning of an enduring business relationship. Dr Jacobsz never missed a board meeting and I will never forget he would always be the first to arrive, often an hour before the scheduled time.

To my immense pleasure not only did Dr Jacobsz believe passionately in transformation but his logical questioning and deep-thinking responses to issues of strategy and acquisitions were invaluable.

Both John and Francois made valuable contributions over many years and at the time of my retirement Dr Jacobsz was still on the board.

Some weeks later my heart was pumping as I walked alongside Tony Worthington and Paul Hutchins and onto the floor of the Johannesburg Stock Exchange. The road that led to this memorable day had been long and fraught with difficulties. A short while before listing I was the sole shareholder in Admark. However, I needed to recognize and demonstrate my deep appreciation to Tony Worthington for his commitment and the Herculean efforts that we had made over the years leading up to our listing.

Leading from the Front

I offered Tony the opportunity to buy 30% of Adcorp for R100 000.

No outsider was allowed to be present at this monolithic institution except on the day that their company was first listed. Admark was the smallest company ever to list on the JSE and I held my breath as the opening bell rang. When I saw our new name, Adcorp, appear on the board I felt vindicated. I was filled with pride. My dream had come true.

We had a champagne reception for our staff and brokers and it took several hours for the euphoria to subside.

The company listed in 1986 with a market capitalization of R5, 4 million. At its peak in 1999 it was valued at just over R1 billion.

Prospectus for listing Adcorp
Profits, prospects and dividends—profits, history and forecast

The following abbreviated table details the audited profit history and forecast of the Adcorp Group for the five financial years ending 31 December 1986 and the six months ending 30 June 1987 together with the forecast profits of the Adcorp Group for the financial year ending 31 December 1987.

31 December R'000	1982	1983	1984	1985	1986	6 months ending 30/06/87	Forecast for year ending 31/12/87
Turnover	4 988	4 726	6 540	5 910	7 950	7 475	12 200
Income after taxation	10	40	90	46	149	289	490
Dividends based on 6 300 000 shares in issue							315
Earnings per share (cents)	0.2	0.6	1.4	0.7	2.4	4.6	7.8
Dividends per share (cents)							5.0
Dividends cover (times)							1.6

Chapter 23

It's all about the people

At the time we listed in 1986 the stock market was booming but the financial experts predicted that the euphoria wouldn't last. It seemed that everyone was being carried away with the belief that there was quick and easy money to be made. The pundits issued warnings to investors not to get their fingers burned. Sure enough the overheated market retreated.

History proves that as any boom nears the end of its cycle there is a last-minute flurry of new listings. Adcorp was on the tail end of this phenomenon and we were among the last of several companies to go public in that year.

The shareholders of many of these newly listed companies suddenly found themselves awash with cash and they rushed like lemmings to buy new businesses. This ill-conceived strategy has been proved time and time again to be a recipe for failure. The acquisitions were often poorly thought out and lacked long-term planning. Predictably they entered fields in which they were totally inexperienced and they got their fingers burned.

Adcorp took the opposite view and we inched forward cautiously in an attempt to prove to investors and financial commentators that our approach was both conservative and prudent. Only 10% of our shares were held by the general public. Under the rules of the JSE this was the minimum percentage necessary, but because of this, we were not under pressure from shareholders to perform miracles. In terms of JSE companies we were minnows, but nonetheless we aimed to build our existing operations and show healthy organic growth. We decided that we would only make an acquisition when we had built a solid foundation.

Our intention was only to look at a company that was in the top drawer, performing well and preferably the leader in its field. Sometimes we uncovered a gem but we didn't manage to convince the owner that we were the right people to sell to and occasionally we let a good opportunity slip. We never wavered from this ideology as we wanted to reassure the investment community that any company we bought was sound and that we were serious players.

We never bothered to investigate any company that didn't already have an annual growth of at least 30%. We weren't overly impressed with the profit history but we wanted to satisfy ourselves that there was sufficient potential for the trend to continue.

Our listing price on day one was ninety cents. Very few of the shares that were in the hands of the public were traded during our first three years in existence and the listing price remained static. As my objective was not to become rich overnight it didn't worry me unduly. I was content to remain patient and was confident that with the right fundamentals in place, success would follow.

My approach to buying a business is somewhat unusual. In attempting to strike a deal the price of the company is never the main thrust of my early discussions. Very often I have found that potential purchasers of businesses tend to become blinded to what they are really buying. They frequently forget that most successful companies cannot achieve success without the help of the people they employ. My philosophy is simple—people first and price second.

The acquisition process is invariably protracted and involves many meetings. In initial negotiations when I refuse to bring up the subject of price the owners are often puzzled. Naturally they are anxious to conclude a broad price agreement before taking the discussions further. I always wanted to be sure that we were on the same philosophical wavelength.

I deliberately push the question of 'how much' to the back-burner.

Instead I quiz the prospective sellers about other issues that are far more important to me. I endeavour to extract every shred of information that I can about the people that have made the business successful. I concentrate on how the owners built the business and why they want to sell and how ethical they are. If I see that the interests of their employees are not at the very core of their thoughts, I back off. If the welfare of their key staff is not central to the negotiations by our second meeting I rarely continue my discussions. If I don't receive a loud and clear signal to indicate that we are in accord I call off the negotiations. If we don't appear to be compatible in our business philosophy I know that there is no point in pursuing the sale. If the seller's vision is clouded, the balance sheet or PE (price-earning) ratios don't amount to anything.

I can think of many instances when we have become embroiled in a bidding war for a company. More often than not our insistence on putting people first, and our genuine interest in the future of the individuals working for the company, enabled us to beat off the opposition. The price was not the ultimate factor that clinched the deal. In the service industry, staff will defect to another company unless it is obvious that you sincerely care about their well-being and that you value their efforts.

There are few things that give me as much personal satisfaction as watching an employee develop skills and grow in stature. When I first met Cornelius Chonco I remember thinking that he was the epitome of a proud, strong, young Zulu warrior. It was in my early days at Admark when I turned my hand to everything and I frequently worked late at the office writing up the books, trying to reconcile our debtors and creditors and creating basic monthly profit and loss records. I was always last to leave the building.

Cornelius was the cleaner and he used to come into my office at around eight in the evening to remove the rubbish bin. Over time we developed an arms-length relationship and I warmed to his amiable attitude to life. We'd chat, usually about inconsequential things. Sometimes I'd ask after his family and from his responses I could tell that he had sound values. One day I said, "Cornelius if you could do anything in the world what would it be?"

"Mr Barry, I would like to work in an office."

I was surprised. I suppose that I expected him to say something like a truck driver or even a minister or doctor.

"If you worked in an office what would you like to do?"

It was an unfair question because Cornelius clearly had no idea what people actually did as they sat at their desks but something about his answer touched me.

I decided that I would try to teach Cornelius the basics of bookkeeping. Although I wasn't a trained bookkeeper myself I had picked up enough over the years to show him how to do simple double-entry bookkeeping. He was enthralled by what he was taught and he was remarkably quick to catch on. I set him a series of simple exercises and each evening he arrived at my office and handed me the completed task. I marked it while he waited and corrected any mistakes. Then he went away with a new set of exercises.

Cornelius was determined to better himself and he proved to be a good pupil. As the months went by we progressed from basic bookkeeping to debtors, creditors and journal entries and by the end of the year Cornelius could already read simple balance sheets.

One evening he came into my office with a doleful look on his face. His eyes were downcast and I could sense that he was troubled. He began to stumble over his words, "Mr Barry, (I'd encouraged him to call me John but he couldn't bring himself to be so familiar) I want to thank you so much. You have helped me to learn accounts work. I have had the chance to better myself. Thank you."

I was taken aback and I waited for some sort of punch line, but it didn't materialize. "I don't know why you are you telling me all this Cornelius?"

"Mr Barry, the job here is finished. My boss said that he is not doing the cleaning here any more. He does not need me so my work is stopping."

"What will you do now? Perhaps your boss can find a job for you somewhere else."

He smiled and shook his head. I was shocked because he'd been progressing so well.

"Cornelius, I can't give you a full-time job here because you don't really have enough experience yet. Still, if you come here at eight tomorrow morning you can start work."

"What job can you give me Mr Barry?"

I had no idea what job I was going to give him to do and I could sense his disappointment, so I added, "Cornelius I can't tell you at the moment, but we will train you for an office job."

His eyes lit up and I could swear that there were tears in his eyes.

Cornelius was first to arrive the following day. He looked a fine figure of a man dressed in his Sunday-best suit. When I saw him standing there so upright, proud and eager I could see that he was indeed realizing his dream and it lifted my spirits. He started by doing the office filing but it barely took him an hour or two so I assigned him to the accounts department. He worked alongside one of our creditors' reconciliation clerks and he picked up the job in no time.

When we moved offices from Joubert Park to Melville many years later Cornelius had worked his way up the accounts department ladder to become a senior computer operator and he was a very valuable member of our team.

Sometimes I think that I derive more pleasure from seeing people blossom and realize their potential than almost anything else. My heart used to lift whenever I stopped for a chat with Cornelius because he seemed so happy and took such obvious pride in his work. I always made a point of doing a daily walkabout through the offices to greet our employees and listen to their problems. I learned that, like Cornelius who had a dream, most people have a deep-seated desire to improve their lot. All they need is to be given the opportunity, recognition and training and they will rise to the challenge.

Years after Cornelius started as a filing clerk his brother Robert joined us as a parking attendant at Melville. He was soon offered a job as an administrative clerk and now they sit side by side in the office.

There have been three women in my life! Perhaps before I lead with my chin I should qualify that statement by saying that I am referring to my business life. The women I salute were my personal assistants at Adcorp!

Shirley Mostert was the first. We worked together for seven years from 1988 and her loyalty and capacity for hard work was quite astounding. As a younger man I was forced to juggle a career with the responsibility of rearing a young family on my own. When I think of how difficult my task was and then compare my struggle with that of Shirley's—she deserved a medal. I enjoyed a great deal of support, but Shirley was a single mother who was battling to raise her three sons alone. When she left Adcorp after seven years it came as a blow to me, but Shirley decided to follow her heart.

She cared deeply about many social issues and in spite of her busy life she managed to spend much of her spare time ministering to people with spiritual problems. She came to me one day and said that she had decided to train as a full-time preacher in Australia. We worked closely enough for me to question her motives and I asked Shirley whether she had given any thought to how she would cope without any support system. She said that her faith would be enough to sustain her and that her mind was made up. She decided to leave Adcorp and travel halfway across the world to dedicate her life to the church. She barely managed to scrimp enough money to pay the air fares to Sydney for her and the boys and after selling all her personal possessions she was left only with a suitcase of clothing.

Shirley left South Africa full of optimism and faith, but her bubble burst when she found that the teaching group she joined had strict and inflexible rules. She was separated from her children, telephone contact was forbidden and she wasn't even allowed out of the mission to visit the nearest town. It left deep emotional scars and soon she began to despair for the well-being of her sons. One day she was at her wits' end and she managed to break free from the mission shackles. She called me in Johannesburg and her distress was obvious. She told me that she was desperately unhappy and penniless. I arranged air tickets for her and she returned to South Africa sad and disillusioned.

Shirley rejoined Adcorp and took up a position as the personal assistant to three directors in the group. Her faith was not shaken and she remained strong, and she is still rendering sterling service to the company today. I hope that one day she will reap the rewards she so richly deserves.

It takes a special person to handle twenty-five things at any one time. 'Multi–tasking' seems to be something that men have never managed to master but Sheila Snelling almost defined the words. I was fortunate to work with her for the three years after Shirley Mostert left for Australia.

Sheila's competence and professional expertise was what really led to her premature departure. I could see that she was just too highly qualified for the job she was doing and it wasn't fair of me to hold her back. Sheila was clearly destined for greater things.

Simeka Management Consulting was a high flying Black Economic Empowerment company that was part of the group and they needed an outstanding personal assistant to support the CEO. Sheila possessed exactly the right combination of commercial experience allied to administrative, financial and accounting skills. With a tinge of reluctance and a good deal of satisfaction Sheila and I parted.

During my last two years at Adcorp I received outstanding support from Merle Miller who worked for me until my retirement.

Apart from these three immense pillars of strength I hold the memories of several other long-term employees with great affection. One such employee is Tina van Rensburg who was everything one ever associates with a typical *huisvrou*. She joined Admark in the early days as an accounts clerk at a time when we only had a dozen or so employees.

Tina was an unwitting party to one of my greatest office embarrassments. During her lunch break I always used to see her knitting furiously and sometimes I wondered if she was making clothes for the whole neighbourhood. One day I walked past the open reception area and bent down to pick up a scrap of paper. There was a tearing noise followed by a deadly silence as everyone stared at my trousers that had been ripped from waist to crotch.

Without missing a beat Tina stepped in to save me, "Quickly, get back to your office, take off your trousers and hand them to me through the door. I'll sew them for you in two ticks."

I retired to my chair and relaxed behind my desk thinking what a stroke of luck it was that Tina was around. I briefly thought how absurd I would look to anyone if they saw me sitting in a shirt with cufflinks and tie, black shoes and socks and underwear.

I dismissed the thought because it was lunchtime and the chance of seeing a visitor was remote. Five minutes later there was a knock on the door.

"Come in Tina, that's marvellous you could mend them so fast."

The door opened and a complete stranger walked in. I'd forgotten an appointment!

"Good afternoon Mr Tyler," I said hiding my embarrassment.

I couldn't stand up to greet him so I just motioned for him to take a seat in one of the armchairs against the wall. He must have thought that I was either very rude or completely eccentric as we continued to conduct our conversation at a distance of eight metres. The longer we talked the more my mind drifted to the way I was dressed. I just prayed that Tina wouldn't burst in and say something like, "John, sorry to disturb you but you left your trousers in my office." I never met Mr Tyler again and

I'm sure that he was happy to get away from his meeting with a rude, gibbering idiot who couldn't string a sentence together.

It is gratifying to see that many of the companies that joined the Adcorp stable over the years have kept their top-flight people in spite of the sweeping changes in this field of activity. It speaks volumes for their leadership, philosophy and positive attitude that they have continued to strive to build those organizations. Even though they have become wealthy and many of them no longer need to work they are motivated to stay at the helm because they still have a burning passion for the company they founded.

Adcorp was expanding quickly. I had to avoid giving any potential seller the impression that they would become a small cog in a big wheel and that we weren't just collecting companies like postage stamps. I wanted them to understand that Adcorp wouldn't adopt a heavy handed influence or take away their independence.

A new seller needs to be approached from an individual perspective as their apprehension about a 'big brother' is perfectly natural. In recognition of this I implemented a measure to counteract any uneasiness and it was designed to give any prospective seller a feel of our organization before they agreed to join us.

I needed to be sure that each one of them was entirely comfortable before taking the final step and I used to say, "This is what I'd like you to do. Here is a list of all of the CEOs in our group. Call any three of them and arrange a meeting. I don't want to influence your choice. They must be three people that you feel comfortable with. Ask them for their honest opinion about how they feel since joining the Adcorp group. See if we have kept our promises and check whether we have tried to make radical changes to the way they think and operate. More importantly ask them whether we have added value to their business."

The response of many potential sellers when faced with this approach was, "You seem so confident I will take your word."

That wasn't good enough for me. "Please don't accept what I tell you as gospel. I want you to see how committed our people are. They may soon be your business partners. Go into the tiniest detail with them and you will find out just how professional they are. When you have satisfied yourself let's speak again."

However comfortable they felt by what I had said the requirement remained; they had to visit and spend time with three company heads.

Chapter 24

Argus—a failure of vision

My negotiations with Steve Mulholland at the *Sunday Times* had gone remarkably well and the discounts we had negotiated encouraged me to approach the Argus Group of newspapers. They were the second-largest media group in South Africa and we were placing huge business with them. I set my sights on achieving a similar deal so with that in mind I arranged an appointment with Jolyon Nuttall.

Nuttall was a senior executive whom I thought would be able to see the logic in granting a rebate to their biggest recruitment advertising customer. In our first meeting I ran straight up against a brick wall when he flatly turned down my proposal. Their policy toward recruitment advertising seemed to be cast in stone.

His uncompromising stance was remarkable because my research revealed everything that I needed to know about the Argus advertising sales strategy. Adcorp bought space based on a price per column-centimetre and in return we were granted the customary 16.5% advertising agency commission but in other areas they were far more flexible. While charging the same column-centimetre rate the Argus Group applied an entirely different scale of discounts to estate agents and personnel agencies and this disparity was both illogical and irritating.

Although this category of advertiser was charged the identical basic rate as us, if they committed to a yearly contract and guaranteed to place a minimum number of column-centimetres, they received a discount of up to 40%!

I threw out a challenge to Nuttall to explain the policy. "We place more than four times as many column-centimetres as any of your other advertisers. I know that for a fact. What earthly logic do you have for dismissing our request for an increased rebate out of hand?"

It was like talking to a tailor's dummy. Nuttall maintained that the Argus had an agreement in place with advertising agencies that governed the commission level. "It's always been that way and it always will be."

"But surely you can distinguish between us and conventional agencies. You give personnel agencies a quarter of our size massive rebates. It's a ludicrous situation."

I was mad as a snake and Nuttall knew it, but I wasn't prepared to let the matter drop. I wrote a stinging letter laying out my arguments and demanding a meeting with the Argus' most senior decision-maker.

Some weeks later I sat down with the top three Argus executives, Jolyon Nuttall, John Featherstone the MD and Hal Miller. Featherstone chaired the meeting and he had obviously been fully briefed by Jolyon Nuttall.

I tried to remain calm and avoid becoming confrontational. I outlined my standpoint and I argued that the Argus needed to make a distinction between advertising agencies and non-advertising agencies but Featherstone jumped in, "This market is split down the middle and will continue that way. It doesn't help you to fight against it. You are an advertising agency—full stop. We cannot and will not increase your rebate."

I kept my powder dry and did not tell them about the rebate I had negotiated with the *Sunday Times* because as far as I was concerned it was a confidential arrangement. The debate went round and round in circles until I finally put it to them.

"Okay, let us assume for the sake of this argument that we were not an advertising agency but an entirely different kind of business, what would your attitude be then? If we said that we'd guarantee to take a minimum number of column-centimetres would we get a 40% discount?"

Featherstone shrugged his shoulders and said, "I can't see any reason why not."

"Mr Featherstone, may I be sure of what you just said? I don't want there to be any misunderstanding later on because I'm going straight back to the office to confirm our conversation in writing. I'm going to tell you that Admark no longer acts as an advertising agency and that we forego the 16.5% rebate. From now on all our advertising will be placed through our personnel agencies. I don't have any problem in signing a contract that will guarantee whatever minimum number of column-centimetres are necessary. That will entitle us to the customary rebate for personnel agencies."

They looked at each other in a somewhat bewildered fashion but having committed themselves they could not back-track.

I went back to my office and immediately dictated a carefully worded letter confirming the meeting and sent copies to each of the three executives present at the meeting. There was a deafening silence from them and a reply was not forthcoming. Their ducking and diving had cost them dearly. For Admark it meant a surge of income to our bottom line.

I instructed the managing directors of each of our regional recruitment advertising companies and told them the good news.

"I would like you to contact your local Argus office. Go there and sign a contract guaranteeing that you will buy the minimum number of column-centimetres necessary to qualify for 40% rebate. More importantly you should be sure to use one of our personnel agencies as a conduit for placing the ads."

With the legally binding contracts from each regional office in the bag I wrote to the Argus Group to confirm the agreements. Our new deal was about to impact massively on our revenue stream and, as in the case of the Times Media Group, at no extra cost to Admark. With no additional effort I estimated that our profit margin would rise from 6%, from a gross income of 16.5% to 30% via gaining a rebate of 40%. It was a stunning breakthrough and I was elated to think that our margins would increase five-fold overnight. We were cock a hoop.

A week after our coup against the Argus, each of our regional managers called me to say that not a single advertisement had appeared in any Argus newspaper but nobody could tell them why. The old proverb tells us not to count our chickens before they are hatched. Now those very chickens that we had counted were coming home to roost!

Our clients, understandably, were rapidly becoming disenchanted because they were not receiving any response to their advertisements. Their vacancies were not being filled and that's not what they expected when they appointed us.

I tried to contact each of the three top managers who had agreed the deal with me at Argus head office to resolve the impasse, but I was totally ignored. I tried writing to complain about their actions. I wrote again and again but they never replied and simply refused to accept our placements.

They had us up against the wall and they knew it. Our lawyers examined our contracts and confirmed that they were watertight but that didn't help us. Even though our legal brains were confident that if we went to court we would win the case they conceded that the process could take months. That was cold comfort to me because we didn't have time on our side. We had to take quick action because it was plain that if we couldn't get our recruitment advertisements accepted by the Argus Group our clients would begin to leave us. Reluctantly I had to climb down on the issue and go back to placing our advertisements through our recruitment agency. It was no surprise when they were all accepted without question.

I cite this highly unethical action as a prime example of commercial bullying. The Argus knew that our business depended on placing our advertisements but the three most senior executives proved themselves to be morally bankrupt. They didn't have the guts to face and confront what was after all a self-inflicted wound. Instead they dealt with it by ignoring us and dishonouring a legally binding agreement.

Years later the old guard changed at the Argus and fresh blood was infused into an ailing institution. I revived my crusade for rebates based on volume and thankfully the management was more receptive. They agreed to my request and it led to every other major newspaper group in South Africa following suit.

Chapter 25

Leading the field

Other than the banks and a handful of other financial institutions, Adcorp was the first intellectual capital company to be listed on the JSE. This distinction created its own set of obstacles.

Investors, financial commentators and bankers found it difficult to measure the worth of intellectual capital. It was far easier for them to judge the performance of a company by analyzing the balance sheet. Before listing, Adcorp's was not in good shape and it was hard to persuade the banks to grant us finance.

Our listing changed the ground rules. We sat in pole position and it meant that any other intellectual capital company with ambitions to list on the JSE would be judged against us. If we performed with excellence it would make it far more difficult for aspirant organizations in the service industry to compete with us. Listing also enabled Adcorp to take a radical step—one that raised eyebrows in many quarters. In 1994 we became the first listed company in which the largest single shareholder was a black empowerment group. At that time very few companies had begun to even think about, let alone embrace the idea.

Our partners were credible, powerful individuals who believed passionately in the integrity of Adcorp's empowerment philosophy. Enriching themselves was of secondary consideration.

The fact that Adcorp was a listed company with members of an empowerment group on the board gave us a significant advantage whenever we entered into acquisition negotiations. This undoubted edge enabled us to stave off competition and increase our appeal to any company we sought to buy.

We began to use our corporate diversity to cross-fertilize our business relationships. We identified those organizations with whom we enjoyed particularly close relationships and we introduced them to the CEO of any new company joining Admark. By opening the door for new companies in the group we were able to add value to their businesses. At the same time we were able to expose our blue-chip clients to other areas of expertise that we possessed.

There was, however, one golden rule from which we never deviated. We did not permit any company in our group to make a sales pitch on behalf of another company for one simple reason; they lacked the passion that they had for their own business. We usually invited clients with whom we enjoyed a particularly strong relationship to our working breakfasts because we felt comfortable to expose them to the CEOs of any new company that joined the group. After that it was up to both parties to pursue the relationship—we merely acted as the facilitator.

Opening the door sounds easy but it bought rich rewards. The key to its success was that it never got out of hand. We restricted introductions to five per year because we didn't want to cheapen or abuse our relationships. Every Adcorp CEO embraced the idea with enthusiasm because they realized that every additional rand of income created extra profit for their company and ultimately pushed up our share price.

M-Net was an example of our ability to widen our relationship. Initially we were only called in to handle their recruitment advertising but ultimately specialist Adcorp companies were also doing their financial advertising and market research. We also managed their JSE listing public relations campaign.

Our complete range of services enabled us to replicate this pattern with many other organizations and at one stage we had business relationships with more than 70% of the top 100 companies.

Top: John stands on the floor of the JSE on the first day of Adcorp's listing, 1986.
Above: JSE Top 100 Award ceremony, 1999. From left: John Barry, Myles (John and Wendi's son), Clare (Myles's wife), Wendi (John's wife), Sean and Delia (John's son and daughter).

Top: The presentation on the day of John's 'retirement' by Vicky Baker, CEO of Simeka/TWS Communications.

Left: Two of the Barry's regular dinner guests at Ingwelala. 'Three spot' (right) and 'Sushi' (left).

Whenever I considered an acquisition it was a fundamental principle that the seller should buy in to Adcorp's philosophy and believe in its growth potential. All our successful acquisitions were based on a PE multiple. The multiple was directly linked to the next year's after-tax profits of the company we were acquiring. Once the new company had joined the group we could add value and that usually resulted in a surge in their existing growth. Another key element of the acquisition formula was that we would value ourselves at a minimum of twice the PE rating of the acquired company. As our PE rating increased I was able to get that ratio to the 3:1 level which impacted very favourably on our earnings per share. However, regardless of ratios, we never bought a company unless it was both strategically and operationally important to us.

Whenever we negotiated the purchase of a new company I always sought to identify and lock in the key people that had been responsible for taking it to the top. These personnel are vital to any business but particularly so in the service industry for without them you have only an empty shell.

Owners were generally happy to sell their business to Adcorp because it enabled them to secure their financial future. However, it wasn't my policy to buy any company outright for cash. Nevertheless when any deal is struck it is essential that everybody is happy. To this end we devised a formula to ensure it.

We signed a contract on the day the deal was consummated. During the next year of trading the seller agreed to achieve a certain pre-tax profit and it was enshrined in the agreement. Assuming that the target was met we paid the seller 50% of the purchase price in cash and the balance was settled in Adcorp shares at the prevailing market price on the date of sale.

I'd found that many of our competitors had a history of losing their key people shortly after the sale of a company was concluded. When this happened, the drive and productivity ceased and the company invariably went into decline. To my mind that was entirely self-defeating and so unlike our competitors, we devised a golden handcuff strategy. To ensure that we didn't lose the services of the key people in the company I made it conditional that the Adcorp shares that had formed part of the payment could not be traded for at least three years. Only after that time were sellers permitted to divest themselves of one third of their shares. In the ensuing two years they could sell the remainder. In this way we ensured that our key people were locked in for a minimum of six years. In practice this rarely happened because of the continued upswing in our share price. The shares held by the sellers continued to rise in value with the result that they continued to hold onto them. As we had fixed the share price on the date that they sold their company they had the assurance that even if the price remained static they would still receive fair value. The dramatic increase in the share price was a real bonanza for them.

Our major investors gained comfort from the fact that senior management held a significant percentage of Adcorp equity and therefore retained a vested interest in the performance of their company and the group.

Investors should ask questions if management doesn't hold significant equity in a listed company because this is the only possible way management can hope to create personal wealth. If they don't have a stake in the company they can only be rewarded through a generous salary package, bonuses or share options. In this case, the incentive to perform with excellence and commitment is rarely as great as when they own equity. However, one must exercise caution because issuing more share options is not the answer. All that does is increase the number of shares and dilutes the value if the correct ratios are not applied.

In designing an agreement there were still a few safety mechanisms that we had to build in to protect ourselves. Every selling shareholder was asked to sign an employment contract stating their salary package. Should any seller understate their package we could have laid ourselves open to the risk of the profits becoming falsely inflated. The net effect of this would have been an increased payout. Every managing director of a new company was required to confirm how much it would cost to replace himself or herself should something untoward happen. After the sale of the business to us their employment contract also stated that their annual package increase would never exceed inflation.

Chapter 26

A test of conscience

I set my sights on another agency after Altolevel rejected our initial bid. At the time it was a relatively large recruitment agency in spite of its small complement of staff. The reason for not naming it will become clear. An unrelated man and woman were the joint owners. She had a loyal personal following of clients although her main role was to run the operational side of the business, while he took care of marketing and client liaison. I was delighted when they agreed to sell and we were able to bring them into the Admark fold.

It seemed like a dream acquisition and profits began to accelerate. We eliminated the need for their administration department by centralizing it in Johannesburg and as a consequence we dramatically reduced our overheads. Furthermore when we added their annual advertising budget to the amount we were already spending we were able to increase our leverage with the media.

The agency first grabbed my attention because they appeared to be highly creative. They consistently gained industry accolades and they scooped a clutch of awards at the Recruitment Advertising Awards Ceremony. About eighteen months after they joined the group I received an anonymous phone call.

"I was at the recent Recruitment Advertising annual awards ceremony and amazingly your new company won about 40% of the creative awards. That's quite an achievement. Perhaps you should investigate the advertisements that won those awards."

I thought about it for a while and dismissed it as a crank call from a jealous competitor but something the caller said played on my mind. He'd said, "Investigate the advertisements that won those awards."

Why did he say it? What did he mean? I couldn't let it drop so I decided to check it out.

The only condition for entry was that any advertisement nominated should have appeared in the *Sunday Times* during the twelve-month period before the closing date of the competition. I gathered copies of the award-winning advertisements and systematically combed every single back copy of the *Sunday Times* during the preceding year. I was shocked to discover that not one award-winning advertisement had actually appeared in the newspaper.

I confronted Jack and asked him to explain the apparent discrepancy.

"Don't worry John. The advertisements were all submitted to our clients for approval but for one reason or another they decided not to run them. The ads were very creative so I thought that it was okay to submit them even though they didn't completely comply with the rules."

I felt sick in my stomach. My conscience wouldn't allow me to accept these fraudulent awards so I called Roy Paulsen the head of Times Media and arranged to meet him to explain what had happened. Although I subsequently developed a close relationship with Roy I didn't know him at the time and that made my confession difficult but necessary. "I wanted to meet you face to face to apologize and tell you how embarrassed I am about the advertising awards that the agency won at the recent ceremony."

Paulsen seemed surprised but allowed me to continue, "I have ascertained that none of them actually appeared in any of the editions of the *Sunday Times*. I can't offer any excuses. All I can say is that I am very sorry that we won the awards under false pretences. I can absolutely guarantee that I had no idea what was going on. It won't happen again and I accept whatever action you decide to take against us."

He didn't express any sign of anger or outrage but thanked me for being honest. A few days later he called to say that the matter was history. The following year the loophole was closed and any entry submitted for consideration in the *Sunday Times* competition had to be accompanied by the original newspaper advertisement.

This incident was a wake-up call and caused me to worry that Jack might not always be operating ethically. They were undoubtedly successful, profitable, and they provided a quality professional recruitment advertising service. The trouble was that I now had reason to question his morals.

Often a problem somewhere in the company is a symptom that all is not well in another area. Therefore I wasn't entirely surprised when I received a visit from his co-MD. She was accompanied by a young, attractive staff member.

What they told me came like a bolt out of the blue. She acted as the spokesman. "John, this is difficult for us to speak about and believe us, we have tried everything before coming to you. We just don't know what to do and you are our last resort. Jack has been sexually harassing the two of us at work for a long time. We have asked him to stop and we have told him that he is a nuisance but he keeps on pestering us."

I felt extremely awkward because I had no experience in handling this type of allegation but I knew that I had no other option other than to confront Jack. He was a mature adult and I baulked at having to reprimand him for unacceptable behaviour but when I did his response was far from apologetic. He angered me by trying to condone his conduct, "So what? The young one is attractive and she's just a typist after all. We can replace her easily but I am the managing director. I'm the one that makes things happen in this company."

I couldn't believe my ears. I expected him to be embarrassed and full of remorse but far from it. I was so incensed that I lashed into him, "I don't care whether you are the office junior or the managing director. I expect you to set the standards and that means behaving in an irreproachable manner toward your staff. What you've done, and even worse, the excuses you have made are totally and utterly unacceptable."

He didn't seem unduly bothered with his dressing-down and certainly made no attempt to apologize for his actions. Nevertheless I thought that I had made my point forcibly enough to resolve the problem. Six months later the two women came to tell me that there had been no change in his behaviour and that he was up to his old tricks. I assured them that I would put an end to it for once and all.

Once I'd taken the decision to get rid of Jack, I had to be careful to follow the correct dismissal procedure and so I put my findings in writing. I advised him that we would conduct a full hearing and offered him the opportunity to call his own witnesses.

When he entered the room the charge was read out but he made no attempt to deny it. Our lawyers had counselled us beforehand and they strongly advised us not to dismiss him on the spot. I briefly reviewed the findings and the following day I wrote a letter of dismissal.

He came out fighting and he threatened to take all the business away from the company. He smugly told me that he had no intention of adhering to the restraint clause in his employment contract because in his opinion his dismissal nullified the clause. I warned him that if he went ahead we would go to court to seek to enforce the restraint.

The upshot was that he brazened it out and in doing so he involved us in expensive legal costs. Then at the eleventh hour he withdrew his action on the advice of his lawyers. We had stayed true to our principles and that was important to me. The value of a watertight restraint clause was indelibly printed in my mind and this valuable lesson taught me how vital it was in any employment contract.

A year later he was back in business and true to his word he recaptured many of his old clients. His business grew by leaps and bounds.

Every year the top advertisers were invited by Times Media on an 'all expenses paid' weekend away. Sometimes it would be to Sun City or even Mauritius or Zanzibar. A year after Jack started his new business I was invited to The Wild Coast Sun along with several of the management team from our recruitment companies.

Before our flight left for Margate the guests gathered at a private function room at the airport for drinks. I happened to turn round just as Jack walked into the room and you could have knocked me sideways! The young, attractive married woman who had complained so bitterly about his molesting of her was now working for his company. To make things worse he had invited her to join him on the weekend and she was clearly enamoured by him. He was totally brazen and when he spotted me he sauntered over and said with a sneer, "You remember (he mentioned the young lady's name) don't you John."

It stuck in my throat and I turned my back on him. It was hugely embarrassing but for the sake of harmony and in deference to our hosts I steered clear of him for the rest of the weekend.

Jack was a rotten apple and he was probably always that way. Like leopards, people rarely change their spots and if you are ever fooled into believing that someone has been rehabilitated think again. Like him, many people appear to change character but the change is usually temporary and is generally forced on them when they are under pressure. This is as true in business as it is in life, but invariably when the threat subsides they slip back into their old ways.

Chapter 27

A brave new world

The release of Madiba heralded a new era for South Africans. The traditional way of conducting business was on the brink of change and whether commercial enterprise either knew or cared, monumental changes in attitude and practice in the country were just round the corner. Any business that hoped to survive, let alone succeed, would be obliged to grasp the nettle. Wealth and opportunity would no longer remain in the hands of the minority and it would be imperative to introduce an enlightened empowerment employment strategy. Not only that, businesses would need to create a significant black empowerment shareholding.

Long before empowerment became fashionable I concluded that unless there is a greater sharing of wealth—a sharing that's roots are grounded in ethics and morality—South Africa would inevitably be confronted with significant difficulty.

When I analyzed the totality of the South African market from the Adcorp perspective I realized that approximately 50% of our turnover was government-generated. I use 'government' in the broadest possible context i.e. national government, provincial government, municipalities, parastatals and many other bodies that would conform with government policy.

Recognizing that new decision-makers were about to move into positions of authority in every one of these sectors, I believed, human nature being what it is, that they would want to deal with people with whom they felt most comfortable.

Adcorp needed to be ready for this. We needed to be in a position whereby we would be able to provide significant professional services during and after this process of transformation. I was confident that this mindset would not only help realize the South African need for a greater sharing of wealth but would also put Adcorp in a strong commercial position.

The first action I took was to dramatically change the shareholding position within Adcorp Holdings Limited. At this time it was my very good fortune to be able to develop a relationship, which in due course became a friendship, with Dr Frederick van Zyl Slabbert. In my opinion, he was and may still be, the most credible white businessman in South Africa. I explained my philosophy and what I wished to achieve to him and sought his assistance and guidance in the creation of a significant empowerment shareholding within our group.

Within a fairly short space of time he was able to bring into one body a group consisting of, among others, Max Maisela, Saki Macozoma, Khehla Shubane and Zanele Mbeki, in her capacity as head of the Women's Development Bank. This group soon became the single largest shareholder within Adcorp Holdings Limited and added great value at all levels to the company. Three of the members of the consortium joined the board and in due course Dr van Zyl Slabbert was appointed chairman of Adcorp Holdings Limited, a position which he still held at the time of writing.

Without his knowledge and credibility I know I would never have been able to put together a team of such quality and integrity.

With the first phase completed the process of empowering all members of the company began. Within a very limited timeframe we had the highest ratio of black employment development at every level, compared to our competitors.

I have no doubt that the primary factor in Adcorp winning the JSE Top 100 award was my pursuit of the strongly held beliefs that I had and the consequential moral, ethical and commercial steps I took. Eventually, as their public profile heightened and they emerged as major players in the South African economy, their commitments became too great and eventually only Khehla Shubane remained on the board.

The new shareholders became hugely influential both politically and commercially and their presence on the board was a major boost. We possessed the perfect balance of professional skills across the service industry spectrum and, allied to genuine empowerment, we stood poised to challenge for government business in the new South Africa.

As time passed and attitudes began to change we needed to rethink our empowerment policy. The early empowerment ventures tended to enrich only a few individuals, but I realized that the empowerment base needed to be considerably broadened. I looked to trade unions as a way to effect the change. We took SARHWU (South African Railways and Harbours Workers' Union) on board because they encompassed Transnet and South African Airways, both of whom were major clients. Next we identified NEHAWU (National Education, Health and Allied Workers' Union) because several of our major clients were in the education and health sectors. After a meeting with representatives of both unions I was encouraged to hear that they were keen to take up equity in Adcorp. The only barrier seemed to be their lack of financial resources.

Sandile Zungu, the head of SARWHU, together with the head of investments at NEHAWU accompanied me on a trip to Cape Town. We made presentations to a number of major financial institutions with the objective of persuading the executives of these companies to make loans to the unions. We needed to raise enough capital for the unions to buy equity in Adcorp. Our proposals met with an extremely positive reception and several large institutions agreed unequivocally to grant the loan. In drawing in the unions we were able to expand our empowerment shareholding in Adcorp from an elite few to a far broader base of people.

During our trip to Cape Town I got to know Sandile Zungu better and I respected his calm and thoughtful approach. After we secured the promise of finance for the shares that SARWHU intended to acquire, I invited Sandile to join our board and with his clear, incisive comments and careful preparation, he became an invaluable contributor at our meetings.

1995 was a year of consolidation during which we did not make any further acquisitions. At the request of Simeka Management Consultancy we increased our stake in the company from 30% to 50%. It was becoming clear that the component parts that went into creating Adcorp were now being reflected in the increasing worth of the company. The combined forces of a genuine empowerment policy and our unrivalled professionalism ensured that we never looked back. Our turnover increased between 1994 and 1995 from R54 million to R79 million and from that point onward we never failed to achieve less than a 50% annual growth in profits.

In 1995 we introduced two additional members to the board—Audrey Mokhobo and Matodzi Liphosa. Audrey Mokhobo's skills as Human Resources Development manager at Eskom, her experience as a member of the Financial Fiscal Commission, and her presidency of the Women's Development Bank brought a great deal of broad-based knowledge and balance. Our team of non-executive directors was further strengthened in 1999 when Dr Danisa Baloyi joined the board. Danisa was a strong advocate of ongoing empowerment developments in the group and added significant value.

Politics

Chapter 28

Inspired to become a true citizen

"You enjoy a fabulous lifestyle. You take everything South Africa has to offer, you've done incredibly well out of this country and yet you hang on to your British passport. Don't you feel bad about it? What stops you becoming a citizen?"

I've lost count of how many times I'd been asked this question. It was couched in many ways, but it boiled down to the same thing. Somehow I always managed to duck the issue, more often than not because I was diplomatic and I didn't want to expound on my political views for fear of giving offence. The truth was that I'd been living happily in the country since I was sixteen and although I constantly searched for a national identity something held me back.

I shouted for the Boks as loudly as anybody at Ellis Park and I always flew the flag for South Africa whenever I travelled abroad. I wasn't holding on to my British passport for the usual reasons. Many people I knew said that they would never give up their foreign passports because they wanted some kind of escape route or safety net if things got too hot. I was different because I loved South Africa passionately and I had no intention of ever leaving. Never; it was my home and my life was here. There was no place on the face of the earth that I'd rather be.

My early years in India, Burma, Pakistan and Egypt had taught me that all men were equal. The government's apartheid policy really troubled me. Even so I was at odds with myself because I knew in my heart that I could never be anything other than a visitor in the country until I took the plunge and applied for South African citizenship.

The release of Nelson Mandela was the trigger I needed. As I watched him walking free I was moved to tears and at that moment I wanted to stand up and be counted. I wanted to be part of a proud new nation and I was determined to be at the forefront of the transformation process.

Days later I sat in front of my lawyer at Werkmans, and announced, "I've come to see you because I want to be a South African citizen. How do I go about it?"

He could barely disguise his astonishment, "Well that's a first for me! Everyone else that comes to see me is trying to get a foreign passport! I can't really help. You'll have to go to the Department of Home Affairs."

All the enthusiasm and hope that accompanied my quest for South African citizenship soon became blunted as I found myself shunted from pillar to post. Red tape seemed to be strangling the Department of Home Affairs. The office at Kaserne was depressing and the clerks that manned the counters were demoralized and downright rude. 'Helpful' was a word that clearly wasn't in any of their vocabularies. When I finally managed to speak to somebody I was sent away on a mission that turned into more of a treasure hunt than an application process. I went on a three-month paper chase and my sheaf of birth and marriage certificates and police clearances grew ever thicker. Then at last, copies of my grandparents' birth certificates arrived in the post from Ireland. I was set to go.

Armed with my file I returned to Kaserne, but any illusions that I had of waltzing through the system were rapidly shattered. The office was crowded and chaotic and the queues stretched out into the street. I looked around helplessly for a sign that said 'South African Citizenship Applications'. I was in cloud cuckoo land—this was where everything from births, deaths and marriages were processed. I looked for the queue that appeared to be a good bet—one that would actually give me a fighting chance of reaching the counter before the office closed. I soon grew impatient and hopped from line to line, but eventually I calmed down and reconciled myself to a long wait. I shuffled forward at snail's pace and I eventually reached the counter. I hoped that by smiling at the lady who confronted me she would look kindly on me. She crossed her arms across her ample bosom in a gesture of defiance. I told her my story and she briefly scanned my documentation. She waved me away irritably and said, "You are in the wrong queue."

I was fuming but tried to remain cool, "Look you may not care, but I've wasted a whole morning in this line. Can you please tell me when your office isn't so busy? Just tell me your quietest time of day and I'll come back then."

She tossed back her beehive hair and sniffed, "Don't ask me. Ask somebody in one of the queues." I drove back to my office in a foul mood and called in my PA.

"Please do me a favour. I've had a frustrating morning at Home Affairs at Kaserne and I've managed to get precisely nowhere. See if you can find out if there's anywhere else I can go that may be quicker."

She came to see me an hour later and hesitatingly delivered the news, "They say that you could try going to Alexandra Township."

I'd never driven into Alex before; there had never been a reason. I'd only ever driven past and I didn't know much about it other than the fact that it was a sprawling township. The thought of applying for citizenship there seemed absurd!

As it happened I located the correct office fairly easily and to my surprise the queues were fairly short. When it was my turn to be served the clerk did a double-take. A white man applying to be a citizen—surely not!

My application churned through the bureaucratic mill and some months later I received a letter informing me that I should attend a swearing-in ceremony at Johannesburg Magistrate's Court. The last time I'd been there was to finalize my divorce!

I was very excited when the big day arrived and I'd even arranged to meet my family after the ceremony for a celebratory champagne lunch.

I didn't really have any idea how to dress or what to take along with me. I wore my best suit and tie just to be on the safe side. My terms of reference for this sort of thing didn't extend beyond watching brief clips in American movies. I could just remember how the camera panned slowly along a row of faces as the people preparing to take the oath placed their hands over their hearts. Some would sob with silent joy, others would beam with pride as the flag was raised and the strains of *The Star Spangled Banner* filled the room. I guessed my experience would be much the same.

I navigated through a labyrinth of halls and passages until I located the small court where the ceremony would take place. A group of people in jeans and T-shirts were milling around. Some sat on wooden benches morosely dragging on their cigarettes. None of them appeared happy—surely they weren't here for the same purpose as me?

A magistrate arrived and ushered us into a tiny courtroom. He indicated that we should stand. Without any introduction he began gabbling his way through the oath of allegiance in a bored voice. He told us to repeat it after him. A wave of emotion washed over me as I spoke the words with pride.

Any hopes that he would follow up with a rousing speech were dashed. I was totally deflated when he began with the words, "Now, for all you new okes ..."

From there his speech went rapidly downhill. If there were judges listening and they had to vote on 'The world's least inspirational address' this dour, bored old magistrate would have scored a perfect ten!

Today I am a very proud South African citizen but I don't walk around with blinkers. I can see many shortcomings both in our government and in our society. We live in the real world and I do not believe for one moment that it is realistic to imagine that we can emerge from our dark past and emerge as a utopian society in a few short years. I come across many sniping individuals in my daily life, people who see nothing good and hang on to the past. When I meet them I always make sure that I present a positive attitude because I have a vision and a passion for the country. Nevertheless, I remain pragmatic and I live my life as it is but I refuse to go along with anything I find unacceptable. I am convinced in my heart that we are going in the right direction but—like all things in life—I would be fooling myself if I think that the process of change will not be flawed occasionally.

At this point in my life I still have a few unfulfilled ambitions but standing out above them all is my fervent wish to spend just five minutes in the presence of Nelson Mandela.

As well as carrying the hopes and dreams of all nations and people of the world he has been my personal inspiration. Madiba possesses the greatest gift of all—unconditional forgiveness. The purity that shines from his face has touched the lives of millions and whenever I see his beatific smile it leaves me profoundly affected.

Chapter 29

Seeing new opportunities

It was time to begin thinking laterally about how we could expand our business. We were dominant in every area in which we operated and we had an enviable list of clients, many of whom were making use of the complete range of our services. I asked myself if there was any avenue that I could explore that would be profitable for us and help to make our existing clients' businesses function more efficiently.

We were placing recruitment advertisements but our clients were handling their own responses. It was an onerous task for them to plough through the mountain of CVs from the hundreds of respondents to each advertisement. It was at the time when many human resources departments were facing increasing pressure from management to downsize.

I realized that because HR departments were finding it hard to cope, there was a brand-new opportunity staring me in the face. If we could find a way of sifting the responses and short-listing the most qualified candidates we would save our clients a great deal of time.

To meet this new challenge we opened Admark Response Handling in 1998 with branches in Johannesburg, Durban and Cape Town. We became the first company to offer this revolutionary service and it strengthened our existing client relations and helped us to garner business from our competitors. Many new clients joined us because it was more convenient for them to put their entire recruitment process under one roof.

A year later we opened Adplan International, a new venture dealing exclusively in financial advertising. The JSE requires all public companies to announce their half-year and end of year results in both the English and Afrikaans national press. Our own portfolio of listed companies proved fertile ground for this brand-new service and many of our clients moved their business to us. Adplan not only helped us to increase our profits but it also strengthened our advertising buying power with the major newspapers.

For two years after listing we maintained a low profile, but 1989 saw our first acquisition when we bought TWS. We broke new ground when we issued additional shares for the first time, but we made it conditional that TWS couldn't trade their 440 000 shares on the open market for three years.

The biggest obstacle to overcome when we opened negotiations with TWS was to convince the owners why they should sell the largest and most successful business in the field of public relations and communications. It was easy to show them the financial benefits, but I needed to persuade them about the emotional ownership ties.

The key executives at TWS were Richard Wagner, a former financial editor of the *Sunday Times*, and Keith Rhodes and Vicky Baker who went on to head up Simeka TWS Communications.

Even though we were on the verge of clinching the deal Vicky was sticking out against it. She alone was struggling with the professional and emotional ties to a company that she had helped to create. One day she challenged me. "Just what do you know about public relations and communications?"

I could read the warning signs and I knew that price alone was not going to be the determining factor in her case and that I would have to appeal to her on another level.

I said, "Well, I have spent a lifetime in marketing and in my mind public relations is one of the facets of marketing. I am not an expert but I think that I have a reasonable grasp of what's needed. I intend to make my contribution when it comes to merging our companies and expanding opportunities and in that way I can add value to both of them. You are the PR specialist so I certainly won't be treading on your toes."

She considered my argument and a few days later shifted her stance from being fervently opposed to the deal to being an enthusiastic participant. The acquisition of TWS has remained the group's most strategically important cornerstone.

In the same year we took a 50% shareholding in Research Surveys and to this day the company is still the largest market research company in South Africa. At the time of our acquisition Research Surveys was owned equally by Butch Rice and Henry Barrenblatt and they made a remarkable team. Butch was perceived by the market to be the research guru while Henry was the front man with outstanding marketing ability and polished client skills. More than twenty years after joining the group Henry is still deeply committed to delivering a quality service and his love of his work and of the company have not dimmed.

In the early days Research Surveys kicked off every month with no billings whatsoever in the pipeline. We'd just run by the seat of our pants and hope that contracts would materialize. We knew that this was no way to continue and so we strove to rectify the situation by creating products to bring in regular income. Research Surveys came upon and then refined and developed a product that came to be known worldwide as the 'Conversion Model'. It was a stunning discovery and proved to be unique in the world of research.

Chapter 30

The Conversion Model

Jan Hofmeyr had a passion for mathematics and statistics and possessed a doctorate in philosophy. Armed with these qualifications Jan spent his days conducting research into religious conversion.

In the early 1980s Jan concluded that religious conversion didn't occur overnight but tended to happen in fits and starts. Until then most theories were based on it being linear.

His big breakthrough was when he developed his 'catastrophe theory'. It had its roots in 'morphology' a branch of mathematics that studies the 'shape' of processes. Jan discovered that the butterfly cusp, a particular kind of catastrophe, may apply to the phenomenon of religious conversion.

Research Surveys had heard about Jan Hofmeyer's work and although his method of analyzing data was new to them, they were keen to test whether his catastrophe theory could be applied to conventional market research. The opportunity arose in 1987 when the Progressive Federal Party called in Research Surveys to assist them with the design of an election survey. To put his theories to the test they asked Jan to develop a questionnaire based on his 'Conversion Model'. The aim was to ascertain whether the process of political conversion was in any way similar to that of religious conversion.

Jan produced a set of questions for the PFP and in the course of his work he became convinced that his catastrophe theory could also be applied to the commercial world, but because of a data-processing hitch at Research Surveys his findings were ignored for nearly eighteen months.

The results came under the spotlight once more when Nedbank contacted Research Surveys in late 1988. Nedbank were considering a merger with the SA Perm, but before finalizing the deal they wanted to find out how it would affect their customers' commitment to them. Research Surveys were presented with the chance to put Jan's theories into practice.

Jan compiled a set of questions and they were test-marketed. When the results came out in 1989 they confirmed that brand commitment and religious commitment were not dissimilar. Six months later the same customers were canvassed and sure enough the 'Conversion Model' proved to be a reliable indicator of who would switch banks and who would not. As a result of his success Research Surveys invited Jan to form a partnership—and the 'Conversion Model' was born.

The study revealed that there are four key elements that enable researchers to predict how close a person is to switching allegiance. The first is to ascertain the extent to which a particular brand matches that customer's needs. The second is how emotionally attached the person is to the brand. Thirdly, how much do other brands appeal? Lastly, how ambivalent or indecisive does the customer become when exposed to the appeal of other brands?

Jan concluded that brand involvement would keep customers committed even if they were dissatisfied. In retrospect it seems a simple discovery, but at the time it was revolutionary.

From the outset 'The Conversion Model' proved to be a strong, validated method of measuring commitment and an indicator of brand switching, but Jan's theory may well have been consigned to obscurity if it wasn't for the entrepreneurial instincts of Research Surveys.

After its success in South Africa, 'The Conversion Model' was launched globally on a marketing budget of just R200 000 and when several companies from USA signed up, Research Surveys realized that they had a winner on their hands. A series of licensing agreements were concluded with top marketing research companies on every continent and today 'The Conversion Model' is marketed in over ninety countries by TNS, the world's second-largest market research company. It is used by almost twenty-five global brands including IBM and Coca-Cola and more than three hundred and fifty product categories have been researched using the method. It has become the most widely used measure of brand commitment in the world.

Adcorp bought a 50% shareholding in Research Surveys for cash and although it was not our usual policy when making an acquisition, this time was different for several reasons.

Some time earlier Research Surveys sold 50% of their company to a group that planned to list on the JSE. Plans eventually fell through and Research Surveys discovered that they had made a bad choice of partner. The group had bought interests in a disparate bunch of companies, none of which had any synergy and as a result they didn't list on the JSE.

After a short round of negotiations we acquired our 50% holding from this group and not from Research Surveys directly. When we structured the deal we didn't want to fund it with Adcorp shares as we did not want to have an uninvolved partner. The cash purchase put us under severe strain but it was a decision that we never regretted.

Over the years Henry Barenblatt and his wife Jane have become close friends and have accompanied Wendi and me to our bush lodge at Ingwelala. The gentlemanly qualities that first attracted me to Henry have been a source of great pleasure down the years.

Chapter 31

Expansion

In 1991 we set up a recruitment advertising operation in Namibia and although it proved to be a relatively small market we had no competition. In no time at all we were handling 80% of the total business in the country. It was a small profit area, but it made a considerable contribution to our media billings.

We also entered the very important Afrikaans-language sector in 1991 by opening Effective Recruitment Advertising. Then we expanded Adplan International's (the financial advertising agency) product offerings and renamed it Adcorp Graphics. Besides continuing to sell financial advertising, Adcorp Graphics acquired the skills to enter the specialized annual reports field. This was good for us as it caught the attention of the senior executives within our client organizations. Annual reports, are a company's premier financial communication and receive the detailed attention of the chairman, CEO and financial director.

We finally managed to acquire Altolevel from Paul Brand in 1991 after protracted talks in the years leading to the sale. In striking the deal we broke new ground and for the first time we used our Adcorp shares to facilitate the purchase. It was something that opened up an entirely new vista for me as I had absolutely no experience in dealing with the major financial institutions. I went to Cape Town feeling rather like David facing Goliath.

Our company seemed very insignificant when measured against Sanlam or Old Mutual so I went straight to Investec, Alan Gray and BoE whom I hoped, as slightly smaller institutions, would lend a sympathetic ear. I was nervous to mention the huge sum of money I wanted to raise but when we got around to talking actual amounts, I was surprised to find that these institutions were prepared to buy however many shares we were ready to offer them.

At first it was difficult to grasp the idea that a ten-million-rand figure wouldn't have fazed them at all. Adcorp's 960 000 shares for a total amount of about R1 million, split between three organizations was small change.

I approached these huge financial institutions with trepidation but was pleasantly surprised to meet with such a positive response to my finance-raising mission. André Joubert of Investec was the first to purchase Adcorp shares and from that point on we developed an enduring business and personal relationship. Until the day I left Adcorp most of these organizations continued to take up whatever equity we offered.

In 1992 our total turnover exceeded R50 million for the first time. In 1993 we changed Admark Response Handling to Admark Personnel Selection because as Human Resources departments in many organizations were further shrunk, and they had less and less time to undertake many basic recruitment functions, we stepped in to fill the gap. Admark Personnel Selection moved up a gear and changed from merely handling applicant responses to delivering a much more sophisticated application vetting service.

The process of interviewing a candidate for a new position is a time-consuming business. To assist our clients we devised a way to screen applicants over the telephone. We asked respondents a series of questions that would help to narrow down the selection and we were able to determine within two minutes how closely the applicant met our clients' requirements.

It didn't matter however specific the wording of any recruitment advert, 80% of all applicants failed to meet the minimum criteria. Applicants were desperate, unemployed or unhappy in their current position and held out some vain hope that in spite of being unsuitable they might get the job. The screening process obviated the need for dozens or in some cases hundreds of face-to-face interviews for one position. Our screening service enabled us to present our clients with a shortlist of applicants within five days of an advertisement appearing in the press. In doing so we broke new ground and further entrenched our client relationships.

Chapter 32

Transformation

After Madiba's release in 1990 the world's perception of South Africa changed rapidly. Soon there was a dramatic surge of international companies wanting to set up operations in the country.

Most of the multinational companies realized the importance of embracing the new way of thinking. They began allying themselves to South African companies that were in the forefront of change and they looked to deal with organizations that had an enlightened and strong commitment to empowerment.

Although TWS was by no means the largest or most profitable arm of our group, it was in many ways our flagship. It was highly visible and it assisted in the strategic planning of many JSE-listed companies and government departments.

When I set about introducing empowerment to TWS I was delighted to find out that the management team were very receptive to the idea. However, I expected to meet resistance as the policy filtered through to the lower ranks and I anticipated that an enormous effort would be required to change the mindset of many employees.

The quick answer to empowerment would have been to introduce a new breed of senior black professionals but in practice it wasn't that straightforward. We couldn't make long-serving white employees redundant in order to accommodate them, and it was unrealistic to expect TWS to absorb an influx of new people to their ranks. The company simply wasn't large enough to accommodate a bloated management structure.

A cornerstone of Adcorp's corporate philosophy had always been to retain the culture of each individual company. I had been told that there were no senior black PR professionals available but it simply wasn't true. In 1994 we launched Simeka PR communications (Pty) Ltd. to go head to head with TWS and at its inception it comprised six highly talented black managers backed by a small support staff.

Our timing was spot on. Coinciding with the opening of Simeka, a tidal wave of new multinationals swept into South Africa. Over the course of the next eighteen months Simeka grew from a zero base into the second-biggest public relations company in South Africa—second only to TWS! Because the wholly black management held 70% of the company equity, every multinational newcomer wanted to deal with them. Soon MacDonald Douglas, McDonald's and many other major organizations gravitated to Simeka.

Simeka were soon victims of their own success. The huge volume of new business threatened to overwhelm them as their resources became stretched. They just didn't have the infrastructure to handle the business that poured in. The company was only represented in Johannesburg and although it was clear that Simeka had a fabulous future in the new South African economy they needed to address the most immediate problem of a weak infrastructure.

TWS on the other hand had offices in all the major centres but it was less well positioned to meet the future challenges. We took the decision to merge the two companies but the dilemma we faced was how to bring together two distinctly different corporate cultures.

Simeka had grown too rapidly and were hard-pressed to cope with the massive inflow of new business. TWS on the other hand had the capacity to absorb new work. The managing directors of both companies came to the conclusion that a merger would be a wise move. They argued that it would be a symbiotic relationship as Simeka possessed the empowerment credibility and TWS the infrastructure.

I resisted the suggestion for quite some time because I envisaged how difficult it would be to merge the very distinct cultures of the two companies. TWS was a traditional and rather conservative organization whereas Simeka was innovative and less formal. Over-riding all these considerations was the thorny question of who would run the show assuming that there was a merger. I also couldn't visualize which culture the new entity would assume.

Six months later the two MDs came to see me again and together they presented their plan. "We have spent long hours thrashing out a solution. We have examined every possible angle and we believe we can make it work. There are immense obstacles ahead but none that we can't overcome together. We have a very clear vision of the way forward. It's going to be a rocky road, but there is absolutely no doubt in our minds that we have to shed our old ideas. We've agreed that there is no other option—we must adopt the vibrant Simeka culture."

Their proposal was so persuasive that I agreed to it. Once we had the principle established there was still the numbers to consider. I set about valuing the component parts so that I could present the proposal to the boards of both companies. Whatever way I did the arithmetic the most generous split in the merged company would only leave Simeka with 15% of the equity and Adcorp with the balance.

In my heart I wasn't happy because I knew that for empowerment to be meaningful a 15% share was not enough. Somehow I had to find a way of increasing the Simeka shareholding to 30%.

I called a meeting with the owners of Simeka and I told them that in my opinion they should own another 15% of the newly merged company. As they lacked the resources to accomplish this I agreed to lend them the required amount. I was acutely cognizant of the fact that the effectiveness or otherwise of the merger would be reflected in the performance of the Adcorp share price.

The loan was provided by the sale of my shares, the proceeds of which I handed to Simeka. The loan was recorded together with the prevailing price of the Adcorp share at the date of the deal. The impelling reason for making this loan was that if Adcorp's share price rose by an agreed percentage over a three-year period, Simeka's debt to me would be reduced. If the full growth target was achieved the loan would be reduced to zero. This is precisely what happened. Adcorp's share price performed so well over the three years that Simeka's several-million-rand debt to me never had to be repaid. Through performance and not through payment, they secured 30% of a much expanded and far more valuable company.

Before the companies were merged to form Simeka-TWS there was not a single black professional at TWS. In the new company more than 50% of the senior consultants were black. The policy was fully vindicated as we began to pick up more and more major contracts including National Road Safety and HIV Education for the Department of Health. The joint capabilities of empowerment and effective delivery that ran from top to bottom in the new company were an example for others to follow.

It was a real feather in our cap when Simeka-TWS were invited to handle the PR and communications for the voter education programme leading up to the second democratic election.

Chapter 33

Building the recruitment and advertising base

In 1994 we acquired Kit Hodge & Associates, a specialist search consultancy based in Cape Town. Admark Recruitment Advertising, Admark Personnel Selection and Effective Recruitment Advertising were already dominant in both the English and Afrikaans advertising recruitment sectors so Kit Hodge fitted neatly into our portfolio. They were able to fill a niche in the market and by adding a search capability we were close to the stage when we could offer the entire spectrum of recruitment services.

In 1994 I sought to optimize our leverage with newspapers by increasing the size of our financial advertising base. I set my sights on Penrose, one of the largest financial advertising companies in South Africa. Penrose was generally thought of as an organization specializing in top-quality printing but they also printed corporate annual reports and handled financial advertising for their clients as an important adjunct.

However, when I approached the MD, Jacky Meckler, it wasn't the printing side that I was interested in. I had my eye on financial advertising and the annual report business.

I originally knew Terry Moolman as the founder and head of Caxton, one of the South Africa's most powerful printing organizations, and during our very early talks I told him that I intended to approach Penrose to buy the company. I indicated that if I was successful I would be amenable to the idea of selling the printing side of the business to him. It made perfect sense to Terry because by doing so it would enable him to expand his printing interests while Adcorp would take over the financial advertising and annual reports business.

My negotiations with Penrose were long and drawn out. Their MD Jacky Meckler, one of South Africa's most famous Comrades Marathon winners, was a very charming man but in spite of meeting him several times we never seemed to make any progress after our discussions. He never contacted me unless I called him. Eventually out of sheer frustration I got in touch with another Penrose board member and asked what news he had for me. From his response it was obvious that Jacky hadn't approached any of the other directors to tell them of my interest in buying the company.

I went back to Jacky and reminded him that as Penrose was a publicly listed company, it was incumbent on him to put any offer from another listed company before the board. I insisted on being allowed to make a presentation. When I did, it came as a surprise to many board members to learn that I had been knocking on the door for so long. At the end of my presentation they assured me that my offer would receive serious consideration.

Before the board had reverted to me with their decision, Penrose held their 1994 AGM and what should have been a routine meeting turned into mayhem. For the first time in South African corporate history, there was a hostile takeover bid. The drama began to unfold when Al Alletzhauser arrived with his lawyer at the meeting. Alletzhauser, unbeknown to most of those present, had an option to purchase the 20% of Penrose shares that were held by Nasionale Pers. There was uproar when he exercised his, voting rights and in doing so he managed to stage a surprise coup d'état. By the end of the AGM the board members had been replaced and Alletzhauser was in de facto control of the company.

The change of control at Penrose made banner headlines but as far as I was concerned the fundamentals in the company remained the same.

Some weeks later I decided to call Alletzhauser to inform him of my negotiations with the previous board and to express my continued interest in Penrose.

We arranged to meet in my office and I outlined my proposals. I pointed out that the Penrose share price had been static for some time and there was unlikely to be any rise in the foreseeable future. I told him that in my opinion it would make sense for both of us if we could come to an agreement. I went on to say that Adcorp shares would probably rise rapidly and the market would recognize our steady growth. Alletzhauser seemed to respond positively to my argument. I offered him the alternative of an outright cash purchase or payment in the form of Adcorp shares. Alletzhauser promised to consider my offer and get back to me in two weeks.

Alletzhauser was a highly intelligent man—capable, committed, presentable, and articulate—and I knew that I'd have to tread carefully. He called me up and said that he was ready to talk.

He arrived at my office late one afternoon for what I assumed would be a meeting to thrash out the finer details of the sale. After exchanging pleasantries for a few minutes he got down to business, "John, I'd like to acquire Adcorp. You've got most of the equity so I'd like you to sell your majority shareholding to me."

I was shaken rigid. What stunned me was that he wasn't offering to buy Adcorp but only my controlling interest. Alletzhauser theatrically pulled out his chequebook and said, "Now how much do you want for it?"

Suddenly I felt a bit-part actor in a movie.

"Al, I can tell you right now that I haven't the slightest interest in selling. Anyway what do you know about Adcorp?"

"Oh, I skimmed through a couple of annual reports. There seems to be room for growth. I can see a few opportunities."

That was it. He'd skimmed through a couple of annual reports. He knew absolutely nothing about Adcorp and he couldn't care less about our people. It was blatant opportunism. As the meeting ended so did my interest in Penrose.

Years later, in a delicious twist of irony, my PA at Adcorp, Sheila Snelling, told me something that I most definitely didn't find funny. She revealed that in a previous life she had worked for Alletzhauser and that she had been his PA at the time he made his audacious offer to buy Adcorp!

Months later Roy Paulsen the managing director of Times Media told me that Alletzhauser had tried the same tactic with him. Times Media was the biggest newspaper group in South Africa while Alletzhauser headed a tiny listed company. He likened Alletzhauser's audacious behaviour to Jonah trying to swallow the whale.

That wasn't the last approach for Adcorp. In 1995 Gary Porritt called me and asked for an appointment. When he arranged the meeting he was vague about why he wanted to see me and only indicated that he had something to tell me that I'd find interesting. As I knew nothing about him or his business I suggested to him that as a preamble to our discussion it would help if he filled me in about his background.

Porritt sounded intelligent and he was certainly charismatic as he calmly sketched the details of his early life in Pietermaritzburg. He told me that he was the son of the Judge President of the Natal Supreme Court and that he himself had qualified as a lawyer. Over time he recalled how he'd drifted in and out of various ventures. He then entered into a rambling account of how he'd tried to corner the entire potato market in South Africa. He presented a very glib explanation of how he'd managed to buy up the total crop of many of the major producers in the country. He explained how his scheme depended on regulating the supply of potatoes to produce markets in such a way that a glut would never happen and the price would remain artificially high. I later found out that he'd omitted one important fact. Sources claimed Porritt never paid the farmers!

After listening to Porritt's life story I was ready to get down to the real business of why he wanted to see me. After hearing the potato story I was somewhat wary but I certainly didn't expect a full frontal assault! Within minutes Porritt attempted the same barnstorming approach that I'd had to fend off from Alletzhauser.

"Let's not waste time, Mr Barry. I am here to tell you why I want to buy Adcorp. I've got a company that I want to reverse into Adcorp and it's the easiest route for me to list on the JSE. Your market capitalization is still quite small so it will also be the cheapest way. You will obviously make a good profit. What do you say?"

It was laughable, but I wanted to let him know how I felt about his proposal, "Mr Porritt, firstly I have no intention of selling, especially to you! You don't buy Adcorp like a potato crop. I am in the people business. I care passionately for them, their lives and their futures and I have a responsibility to them all. Thank you for coming but we have nothing to discuss."

My brush with Porritt lasted perhaps half an hour. Today Porritt is fighting for survival. The financial director and auditor of his listed company, PSG, have turned state witnesses against him in a case that may end up costing shareholders hundreds of millions of rands. The state is attempting to unravel a complex set of acquisitions and inter-company transactions that lie hidden in a maze of deception. At the time of writing Porritt was awaiting trial and it is my fervent hope that he will be bought to justice.

Simeka

Chapter 34

The birth of a giant and the creation of Simeka

Early on in our development I recognized that a very clear division existed between the English and Afrikaans recruitment markets. We moved to cater for both sectors by establishing separate specialist companies and for many years we had all bases covered. In 1995 we found ourselves having to rethink.

The ANC had been elected to government and a dramatic change in the conventional method of recruitment was imminent. It stood to reason that within a very short time most government departments and parastatals would be staffed and managed by black personnel.

It was logical that the new decision-makers would seek to do business with organizations that were not only genuinely empowered but also possessed the professional skills to do the job. We needed to move swiftly and decisively to meet the challenge.

When we created Simeka Recruitment Agency it had a significant empowerment and strong black management. Simeka Recruitment Agency became the only company with strong enough credentials to home in on the exploding empowerment market. Almost immediately after its formation; Simeka was appointed to handle the national government recruitment account and this was quickly followed by contracts with the provincial governments of Gauteng, Northern Province, KwaZulu-Natal and a host of parastatals. Within two years Simeka was catapulted into second place in the South African recruitment advertising stakes and by the end of the year, Adcorp companies were ranked in first, second, third and fifth place among the nation's recruitment advertising companies.

By this time Adcorp was the major, if not unassailable, leader in the South African recruitment, communications and market research industry but there was still one piece of the jigsaw missing. My final step was to move into management consulting. I felt if we had that cornerstone in position, the group structure would be complete. However, the way it presented itself was somewhat obscure and unexpected.

In being awarded the Gauteng government's recruitment business Simeka was made abundantly clear that transformation within the administration's ranks was an urgent priority. Consequently, I spent many hours with Gauteng's Commissioner Walter Mbeti who had been appointed to the position by Mandela. Walter outlined his vision and together we began working toward a complete overhaul of the way recruiting had been tackled in the past.

Radical transformation had to occur rapidly and at all levels. To comply with local government requirements I realized that it would be necessary for us to change our approach as well. It would no longer be viable to place advertisements in newspapers such as *The Star* or *The Citizen* because we just wouldn't get our message through to our target audience. Most job seekers in the lower levels didn't read the newspapers! We put our heads together and decided to break from tradition and to advertise vacancies on outdoor hoardings, bus shelters and on radio spots. It proved to be a hugely effective way of recruitment.

In the weeks we spent formulating strategies and policy, Walter and I became close friends. Therefore, it didn't surprise me when he took me into his confidence about two bright young stars in the government. The men in question were Barry Fraser and Robinson Ramaiete. Walter told me that both had been closely involved in the transformation process but they were about to resign and open up a management consultancy. He hinted that Adcorp could be an ideal home for these two exceptional individuals.

Neither Barry nor Robinson possessed any experience in a commercial environment but they immediately struck me as having all the right qualities. They were both young, bright, qualified and passionate and they truly understood the problems that confronted government. More importantly they had a clear vision of how the problems could be solved.

Thus it was in 1996 that Simeka Management Consulting was born. Adcorp raised the start-up capital and at the start we held 33.3% of the equity while Barry and Robinson held the balance.

Traditional and well-respected management consultancies relied on ready-made solutions to solve a host of routine business problems. What they didn't possess was an off-the-shelf answer to transformation. That required a completely new perspective and a rare insight into the machinations of government. That was where Barry and Robinson held the aces but because they were commercially inexperienced I didn't put pressure on them to perform to the same level as the other companies in Adcorp. Time was on their side and it was essential that they were allowed to develop slowly, carefully and correctly to ensure that Simeka Management Consulting would one day emerge as a consultancy of real consequence.

Next, we managed to reel in the last really big fish and it very definitely tested our ability to absorb and digest it. We bought Quest Personnel, the second-biggest personnel agency in South Africa. The founders had built the business over a number of years and by the time they decided to sell they had forty-four branches scattered around the country.

By acquiring Quest we cornered the recruitment advertising market and we were a substantial force in personnel selection and staff search and screening. However, purely in terms of size, personnel selection stood head and shoulders above the rest. To put it into perspective there were twelve recruitment advertising agencies in South Africa but there were over 1,500 personnel selection agencies, even if many of them were one-person shows.

With so many competing for a slice of the recruitment cake the only way that many of them could distinguish themselves from the pack was to operate in a specialized niche. It would have been folly for a smaller agency to attempt to be all-embracing and it made perfect sense for them to specialize in placing personnel in a narrow category such as catering staff, engineering or sales people. To place a CEO or financial director required a different technique and greater sophistication than the skills needed to engage a truck driver or a chef.

I needed to get a complete overview before deciding on my next move. I conducted an analysis aimed at segmenting the market and establishing how many broad sectors existed. Although it was not an exact science I determined that there were about fifteen categories of staff that personnel selection agencies were specializing in. Some of course were far larger than others because the need for administrative staff or shop assistants was far greater than the requirement for consulting engineers or industrial chemists.

Once I had identified these segments, I researched via our key clients, the best, and most professional operations in each specialist segment, I then set my sights on bringing them into the Adcorp fold.

1996 saw our single biggest growth period. Turnover jumped from R79 million in 1995 to R212 million the following year. Profitability more than trebled as it shot up from R2.6 million to R7.9 million. In the past our gearing had been a source of concern both to myself and to outside shareholders but from a high of 240% in 1993 it dropped to 204% in 1994, 187% in 1995 and finally to 54% in 1996.

We continued to look for more quality personnel agencies that we could slot into our existing businesses. During 1997 Adcorp bought three more agencies. The largest of these was Emmanuels, a company founded by Litsa Roussos. She possessed a delightful, open, bubbly personality; her enthusiasm was boundless and her passion for life, her staff and her clients was infectious.

Unbeknown to me when I opened negotiations, Litsa had already been courted by one of our major competitors, Educor. I particularly wanted to bring Emmanuels into the group because of the reputation that their specialist medical division enjoyed. When the dust settled and we signed the deal, Litsa confided to me that Educor had tried hard to persuade her to sell. After she told me this, Litsa shot up in my estimation because at no time during our negotiations did she use it as a bargaining tool to squeeze out a better deal.

The other two companies that joined the Adcorp stable that year were Premier Personnel and Grey Appointments, an agency that specialized in placing financial directors, accountants and bookkeepers.

Optimal Advertising was a dynamic recruitment advertising agency that emerged rapidly and successfully in Durban. I was delighted to bring them on board because when we added their considerable advertising spend in Natal to that of our existing companies we further increased our bargaining position with the newspapers.

By centralizing our administrative functions we pushed up our overall profitability and it grew by nearly 100% to over R14.5 million, while our gearing dropped to an encouraging 19%. By this time Adcorp was really beginning to flex its muscles. We had 75% of the recruitment advertising market in Durban, 80% in Cape Town, 80% in Namibia and by far the largest share in Gauteng.

By the mid-nineties, outsourcing was a buzz word on every South African business person's lips. Executives began to examine and redefine their core business and in the process they often found that they could dispense with many permanent staff members that were on the periphery of their business.

It was clear that many job functions could be handled adequately by outside contractors. By shedding these employees not only were companies able to significantly reduce their salary bill but far more importantly they could concentrate on doing what they did best. They also realized that by reducing the number of permanent staff they could make considerable savings on social benefits.

To begin with they outsourced jobs such as cleaning, messenger services, deliveries and catering. They called on outside companies to provide those services and as a result they were able to shift responsibility for holiday pay, medical benefits and pensions to a third party. Eventually, owners and managers of businesses realized that almost every job from data processor to engineer could be outsourced

Almost overnight, recruitment agencies that had geared their businesses to meet the demand for a semi-permanent type of employee blossomed. Quest was one of the first agencies to recognize the potential of outsourced employees and soon Quest Outsourcing became their largest division. Many organizations contracted staff on a long-term basis to help them fulfil contracts but they were effectively Quest employees. When any particular project came to an end Quest was able to withdraw their staff and redeploy them elsewhere. This had immense benefits for any company using Quest services because they no longer had to staff for peak periods and they didn't have the problem making staff redundant when a particular project came to an end. Quest, in recognizing the trend turned the outsourcing arm of their business into their largest profit centre.

In assessing the changing market I could see clearly that nursing staff were the perfect example of how effective outsourcing could be used. In 1998 Adcorp acquired Charisma Nursing Services a company that specialized in recruiting and placing nurses in private hospitals. When we assumed control of the company it had five hundred full-time nurses in hospitals dotted across the Witwatersrand.

Charisma proved to be an outstanding acquisition and it grew dramatically under the management of an ex-Sandton Clinic matron who possessed a keen insight into the requirements of both the nursing staff and the hospitals. She brought tremendous energy to the business and Charisma expanded so rapidly that by 2000 there were over six thousand nurses on the payroll.

The rapid growth of this kind of business resulted in a situation where hospitals found it virtually impossible to employ nursing staff directly. Because many hospitals had closed their administration departments many of them turned to Charisma to provide them with their entire nursing and nursing administration staff.

Unlike many of our competitors Adcorp followed a policy of treating every member of its full-time outsourced staff as permanent employees. They are placed on the group pension fund and medical aid scheme and they receive standard annual leave pay.

By the end of 2000 we had 1 500 employees working for Adcorp and a further 13 500 people were employed through Quest, Charisma and Emmanuels. From nurses to technical support staff, our outsourcing division became the fastest growing and most profitable business.

There is little doubt that outsourcing will continue to grow and in the future it will present huge opportunities across the board. However, the recipe for success as far as the recruitment business is concerned will be the ability to recognize where the demand for staff exceeds the supply. Only by controlling the supply in sectors such as nursing will it be possible to avoid being drawn into a price war.

I studiously avoided entering any segment of the recruitment market that was either too small or vastly overtraded. Nevertheless in 1999 when the opportunity to buy Peak Personnel and DAV Personnel presented itself I jumped at the chance.

DAV Personnel was founded by Ingrid Kast, one of the most passionate and enthusiastic company heads that I have had the good fortune to meet. I have never seen such a close relationship between an agency and its clients, and the DAV commitment to training is awesome. Their investment of money, time and energy is reflected in the unswerving loyalty of Ingrid's staff and their sheer professionalism of service to their clients.

Ingrid began her business by recruiting personnel for German companies based in South Africa. These companies needed technical and engineering support skills and there was no significant rival to cater for this specialized market. Since our acquisition the company has demonstrated unparalleled growth and without doubt DAV has emerged as the jewel in the Adcorp crown.

I have frequently been asked for the secret of Adcorp's success, as if I had some kind of Midas touch that could be replicated. I answer with just two words—'Exceptional management'. All our companies had this quality.

It is a matter of great personal satisfaction that to this day many of the companies that I acquired are still run by the people who founded them. It is this continuity that has enabled them to retain the unique culture that made them so attractive in the first place.

Adcorp

Chapter 35

Bidding for Kelly Girl

When I heard that Neville McKay, the founder of Kelly Girl Personnel, was on the verge of retiring and selling his company I decided to enter the bidding process. Neville built the business from scratch and it rose to become the largest South African personnel agency with branches in almost every town and city. Interestingly, contrary to popular belief, Kelly Girl in South Africa has no connection with the worldwide brand. Years back Neville was smart enough to register the company name and trade under its banner and ironically he didn't even have to pay a cent in royalties!

When we began to delve a little deeper into the company accounts we surprisingly discovered that Kelly Girl was not nearly as profitable as we'd assumed. On closer inspection, I concluded that the rather thin margins could probably be ascribed to the fact that Kelly Girl dealt mainly in the provision of administrative staff. This competitive area of the business is notorious for delivering lower profits.

Initially five companies expressed interest in acquiring Kelly Girl, but they sought to reduce the number of bidders. Finally the serious contenders were reduced to three and although I wasn't able to confirm which other companies were in the race, I guessed they were Educor and Bidvest.

The method employed to sell the Kelly Girl organization was groundbreaking in South Africa as normally a company of such stature would work through a merchant banker. In the case of Kelly Girl it was to be sold via a bidding process. To ensure transparency they charged their auditors with the task of overseeing the due diligence. Each potential buyer was permitted access to any Kelly Girl documentation under their supervision.

Having completed the due diligence I elected to withdraw from the race. In many ways I had regrets because I firmly believed that Adcorp was the best placed of all the bidders to absorb the Kelly Girl organization into its ranks. In the end I held back for a very sound reason.

I was comfortable with the numbers, but it worried me to discover that Kelly Girl appeared to treat the welfare of their employees as a low priority. They had a huge staff complement, but there was a total absence of either a pension or provident fund. If we had integrated Kelly Girl into the ranks of Adcorp it would have been necessary to rectify this anomalous situation and in doing so we would have created an enormous drain on the future profits of Kelly Girl.

Ultimately Educor won the bid and took control of Kelly Girl, but when I heard the price that they paid I was sceptical about their ability to sustain the already slim margins. It was no surprise to see that in the ensuing few years Educor's profits declined significantly.

Chapter 36

The ultimate accolade

In 1999 Adcorp won the prestigious JSE Top 100 award. We were the first service-based company to do so and it was a proud moment for me. It was undoubtedly the pinnacle of my career and I viewed this public recognition of our success as the springboard for the future.

The sole criterion for determining the winner was 'Return on Investment'. In a five-year period Adcorp had achieved an annual compound growth of 79%. An inscription on the award read, 'An investment in Adcorp of R10 000 in 1995 was, in 1999, worth R181 437'.

In business terms Adcorp had grown from a very small base to become a big company and my maxim for forging into the future was, 'We have built the ground floor—now let's build a twenty-storey building on top of it'.

Although the company won the accolade it would perhaps have been far more pertinent to examine the dynamic management and excellence of our employees. It is they who really deserved the honour.

I should emphasize that Adcorp is merely a vehicle that the financial community can understand and analyze. It is the companies within the group that have helped to plot its success. My message to all the Adcorp managing directors was that they should continue to operate in the same vein and use the same emotions and philosophies that they had when they founded their companies.

Should the Adcorp board ever fall into the trap of thinking otherwise and imagine that head office, and not the operating companies, are the centre of the universe, it will signal a downhill slide. Adcorp, to use an analogy, exists as the oil on the wheels. Its purpose is to create a vision and develop strategy.

Sometimes I find it rewarding to glance over my shoulder. It surprises me because when we listed on the JSE in 1987 the company was valued at a mere R5.6 million. Just twelve years later we captured the JSE Top 100 Company Award and Adcorp was valued at R1 billion. Between 1991 and 1999 we averaged compound earnings per share growth of over 50% per annum.

Turnover millions

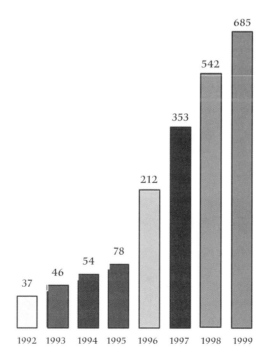

Leading from the Front

Operating margin percentage

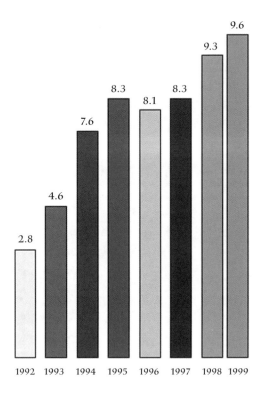

Adcorp

Operating profit in millions

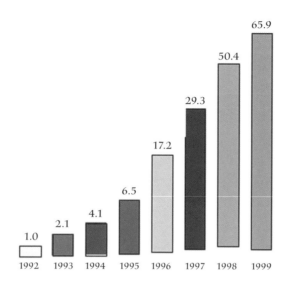

Earnings per share (cents)

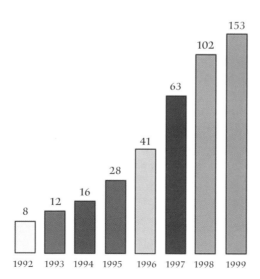

Chapter 37

Battles with health

"I think you should phone your wife. Tell her to bring your pyjamas. I am going to operate in the morning."

I can still hear the doctor's words ringing in my ears. To be honest I was shaken rigid. My first thought was, "There goes our holiday in Mauritius, our kids will be so disappointed."

It was just a small lump on the back of my leg, something that Wendi had reminded me to have checked out, but certainly nothing to worry about.

Within an hour I found myself in a hospital ward for the first time since my horrendous motor accident. The other bed in the ward was occupied by a youngish chap in his mid-twenties who lay with one arm attached to a chain that was hanging from the ceiling. I sat around awkwardly not knowing whether to keep quiet or strike up a conversation when he let out a series of strangled moans. I thought that it was strange to see him smoking but dismissed it. Suddenly he dropped his cigarette on the floor and croaked out, "Hey, china, help me man. Pick up my fag."

He pressed the emergency buzzer and a couple of nurses came running,

"Jeez, help me I can't stand this pain. Can't you bring me painkillers?"

The nurse ignored his request and told him they were too busy for his nonsense. They certainly didn't show the kind of sympathy I'd expected.

Minutes later he detached himself from the chain and disappeared to the bathroom. He came out with another cigarette drooping from the corner of his mouth, clambered back into his bed and pressed the buzzer again.

A nurse arrived at his bedside, hooked his arm up and took away his cigarette. This charade was repeated several times while I sat by getting increasingly nervous about my impending operation. Finally Wendi pitched up with my gear. She was in a highly emotional state after watching the performances of my ward partner. She turned to me and said, "John, I can't stand this chap's antics. The doctor has said that you've probably got malignant cancer. The last thing you need is this stress."

I assured her that I'd be fine and had her go home early. The cigarette and buzzer routine was repeated several more times with the nurses becoming more and more agitated. When the fellow's mother arrived at visiting time he launched into a tirade against the nursing staff, "Mom, they don't care about me. I am in terrible pain and they just ignore me."

His mother was so distraught that she left the ward early, tears streaming down her cheeks. As soon as visiting hours ended he unhooked his arm and wandered out of the room with a dressing gown draped over his shoulders.

He'd been gone about ten minutes and I began to worry that something had happened to him so I pressed the buzzer and the nurses came rushing in.

"Look, I'm sorry, I know this guy has been bugging you but he left about ten minutes ago and I thought I'd better tell you."

Fifteen minutes later the nurses bought him back to the ward. They had found him outside trying to phone for a taxi!

The surgeon that diagnosed the lump in my leg just a few hours earlier strode into the ward and began berating him.

"We've all had enough of your bloody nonsense. I'm telling you this for the first and last time. If you press the buzzer, unhook your arm or light up another cigarette I will call the police and ask them to throw you in jail. He turned to me and said, "I'll tell you this poor chap's story, but first let me move you to another ward."

Once moved he continued, "It was 1981 and South African troops were forging deep into Angola. This chap was engaged with the army up there. His job was to look after the horses that the defence force were using during the reconnaissance missions. He told me that the horses often returned in a terrible condition after becoming snagged on barbed wire."

The surgeon went on to recount how the young man who was his patient had to administer pain-killing injections and stitch the wounds. To dull the mental anguish he'd begun to inject himself with the same drug that was used on the horses and over time he had become hopelessly addicted. He'd been admitted to hospital after slicing off four of his fingers in an accident. Mercifully his colleagues had the presence of mind to bring the severed fingers to hospital in an ice pack and the surgeon had managed to save them. His problem was that the regulation dose of hospital pain-killers didn't do the trick. They just weren't strong enough.

Next day the surgeon cut out a malignant melanoma from the back of my leg. He patched the wound by taking a skin graft from my other leg. I consoled myself with the thought that it would have been worse if the melanoma was on my body. Three weeks later I was back in hospital, but this time my appointment was with a heart surgeon. He told me rather alarmingly, "I'm going to have to separate your leg from your body. That means clamping off the main artery into your leg."

I was relieved to realize that he didn't have amputation in mind. He hitched me up to a heart monitor and my leg was pumped with chemotherapy drugs. For months there wasn't a hair on my entire body! It took another three years before the surgeon pronounced me cancer-free.

Two years later I had my first heart attack and until you've had the first of anything you don't have any experience of how to react. In my case the circumstances were rather dramatic.

We arrived at our Ingwelala cottage to spend the weekend in the bush with our friends David and Sally. It was late on Friday afternoon and we were anxious to go on game-drive before dark. We grabbed a few snacks and packed the drinks in a cool box and set off in the Land Rover. I knew I didn't have much time before it got dark so I drove straight to Elephant Pan.

There was a water reservoir about fifty metres beyond the waterhole. Weeks before it had been lowered to allow the elephants to drink out of it. For some reason elephants prefer fresh reservoir water rather than water that has been pumped into a waterhole. Before the reservoir was lowered they used to stand on their back legs and dangle their trunks over the edge to get at the water source.

Elephant Pan is surrounded by dense bush and it certainly isn't a safe spot to get out of the vehicle for sundowners. I nipped round to the back of the Land Rover to fetch the cool box when I suddenly noticed that Wendi and the others were sauntering toward the reservoir. There is never a safe time in the bush but at dusk the risk of encountering predators on the hunt is very real. I didn't want to appear alarmist so I hurried over to the reservoir. Wendi was deep in conversation with David and Sally and was explaining how the changes to the height of the reservoir helped the elephants. I urged them to rapidly get back to the safety of the Land Rover.

We had just settled down to enjoy our sundowners when a pride of eight lionesses came prowling past just yards from the vehicle. They crouched at the waterhole and began to slake their thirst. We watched for more than half an hour before they stealthily moved off into the night. It was a close call and we had broken a golden rule—never take the bush for granted.

The next morning I needed to go to the camp office. It was blisteringly hot as I left the office to make my way across to the shop. I'd barely gone a couple of steps when I was overcome with the heat and I just slumped down on the path in the shade of a small thorn tree. Suddenly I felt a vice–like tightening across my chest and although I didn't recognize it at the time I was suffering a heart attack.

Within minutes a crowd gathered and the manager took control of the situation. He called Hoedspruit Air Base and they dispatched an ambulance. I was bundled into a vehicle driven by a staff member and we set out on a very bumpy fifty-five-kilometre ride over a badly corrugated dirt road.

Hoedspruit Air Base was the nearest facility to Ingwelala that was able to deal with a serious medical emergency. The base was equipped to handle major disasters and in many ways I had the government to thank for saving my life. My attack happened at the height of cross-border hostilities and the hospital at the base could have handled a military disaster on an epic scale.

I was shoved into the passenger seat while the manager had his back to the dashboard. He was pumping my heart furiously. My head was in a spin and I can remember him screaming, "Hang on, hang on. Oh no, his bloody heart has stopped. His pulse has gone!"

We were halfway to Hoedspruit when the ambulance coming in the opposite direction pulled up beside us. A member of the medical team sprang out and immediately gave me a morphine jab. I know better now and I have a chain to denote my allergy to the drug!

I was stabilized at Hoedspruit while the medics called Nelspruit for a medevac helicopter. As I was being carried aboard Wendi arrived and just touched my hand briefly before we took to the skies. At Nelspruit I was transferred to a twin-engined aircraft and flown to Lanseria.

Wendi drove with our friends first to Hoedspruit and then to Nelspruit, only to find that I was almost on my way to Johannesburg. They were absolutely exhausted and spent the night in Nelspruit before driving next morning to Milpark Hospital in Johannesburg.

Some days later I was given an angiogram and learned that no major damage had been done. It was a massive scare and it certainly could have happened in a more convenient location. I have learned after three subsequent heart attacks that if you hope to survive you must pray that there are good medical facilities close by!

I had a steady stream of well-wishers and the area around my bed looked more like the local fruit and flower shop. True to form my old pal Germain Marquis arrived armed with a bottle of vintage red wine. It was mid-afternoon but Germain didn't set too much store by conventional visiting hours and charmed his way past the duty nurses. He produced two crystal glasses, popped the cork and we celebrated my survival!

Sally, the wife of my dear friend Tony Worthington, together with a group of friends came to see me one evening. She sat at the end of the bed but her eyes never left my heart monitor. She seemed fixated by the blips dancing across the screen and started to glance across at the monitors beside the beds of other patients. Soon her head was bobbing back and forth like a metronome as she attempted to compare pulse rates. When it was time to leave she took my hands in what I took to be a compassionate gesture. She kissed me lightly and pressed my hands to her ample breasts! My heart skipped a beat.

"Good, very good, I just had to see if that had any effect on your pulse rate!"

By December of 1996 I'd taken a firm decision to slow down. I planned to withdraw gradually from the rigours of daily life at Adcorp and begin the search for my successor. I hoped to travel a little and spend more time in the bush. The company was on a very firm footing and there was no need for me to work so hard anymore. As part of the scaling-down process we decided to sell our house in Bryanston. It had provided us with so many wonderful memories over twenty years and we were sad to leave. We moved into a beautiful new home in Khyber Rock close to the Johannesburg Country Club. Everything seemed to be slotting neatly into place. Two days after moving into our new home, at three o'clock in the morning, I had yet another heart attack.

I was woken by the same massive chest pains. Wendi called the emergency services and they were on the spot in ten minutes. This time I was rushed by ambulance to Sandton Clinic. Once again I came away relatively unscathed. Doctors doubled the dosage of heart and blood pressure pills and to this day I pop around a dozen a day.

In 1997 I suffered a stroke although I wasn't certain what had happened at the time. I was driving to work in Melville and, as usual, I called my PA from the car. I wanted to run through my schedule for the day with her but when she came on the line I began to slur incoherently. I knew enough to guess that something serious was happening to me and I somehow managed to get her to understand that she should wait for me outside the offices and rush me to Sandton Clinic.

My GP, Joe Skowno, had been alerted and was on hand to check me into a private ward. Joe was quite calm about the whole thing and assured me that it was fairly common to have a stroke while sleeping or soon after waking. Within a day I felt back to normal but Joe arranged for a series of tests to ascertain the damage. I was manoeuvred into a narrow capsule for a brain scan and while I was lying there I tried to do mental exercises to see how badly I'd been affected. It could have been far worse as only one side of my brain was damaged.

Regrettably it has had a lasting affect on my short-term memory. Nowadays I get embarrassed if I meet somebody just a day after I have been introduced but can't remember meeting them or what I discussed. The problem is that this memory loss is erratic and very selective in what it chooses to forget! I have accepted this as part of life and only hope that I haven't offended too many people along the way!

The brain damage manifests itself in other ways too. My thought process is clear but nowadays when I attempt to transfer my thoughts to paper I am prone to writing gibberish. As this glitch begins to worsen I rely more heavily on my PA to screen everything I commit to writing.

I sailed through the next few years in near-perfect health until I was struck down with my third heart attack. Wendi was away in Ingwelala for a short break with a group of close friends and I was alone at home. At about four in the morning the chest pains began. This time I knew the signs.

I grabbed for the pills and swallowed half a dozen in quick succession. Wendi is a highly organized person and she would immediately have known who to call for help. I didn't have a clue what to do except that I would probably need to get to hospital fast! I hoped for a minor miracle and I thought that if I stayed calm and went to lie down the pills would kick in and I'd be fine.

Two hours later I crawled to the phone and called my good friend Craig Tobitt. "Please get here quickly, I think that I've just had another heart attack and Wendi is away!"

Craig arrived within fifteen minutes but he was visibly shaken. His wife Erina had armed Craig with a photocopy of a map that he clutched in his hand. I was surprised because I would have assumed that Craig was quite familiar with how to get to Sunninghill Clinic.

"Erina has called Sunninghill. Your heart surgeon Jeffrey King is away. His locum only operates from Olivedale so we've got to get there, but I'm not sure of the way!"

We screamed through the early morning traffic and before seven I was hooked up to a heart monitor. It was becoming a bad habit!

Again I cheated death and thankfully the grim reaper wasn't ready for me!

If they handed out medals Dr Jeffrey King, my cardiologist, would win the gold. Anyone who saves your life only once is entitled to be called a friend but Jeffrey has saved me a few times now. Our relationship that began in the surgery and continued through the operating theatre has today developed into a firm friendship.

In his spare time Jeffrey is a keen and accomplished photographer. He shares my great love for the bush and he is particularly passionate about photographing leopards in the wild. When I go for my check-ups we usually end up talking about wildlife.

Jeffrey is a fairly laid-back young fellow and he loves pop music from the '60s. He is a big hit with the nurses because he often brings a mini sound system into the operating theatre and performs operations to the sound of the Beatles and other stuff from that era. I was laid out on the trolley table waiting to be wheeled into the theatre for an angiogram. As I was lifted on to the operating table I heard Jeffrey asking one of the nurses, "Bet you don't remember where this one comes from?"

Quick as a flash she replied, "Oh yes I do. It was top of the charts when I was in matric."

I was a little tense in anticipation of the angiogram and I clutched at the table. Seeing my taut muscles and clenched fingers, one of the nurses held my hand. Her mind must have drifted and within moments she was tapping my hand along to the rhythm of the music!

In July 2004 I was back again. I'd suffered my fourth heart attack. One of the nursing sisters recognized me and we had a laugh about the impromptu 'angiogram rock concert'. I left the hospital a day or so later not much the worse for wear, but with a handful of new pills.

Between my heart attacks Joe Skowno discovered that I needed a hernia operation. He sent me to see a specialist in Sunninghill who confirmed the hernia, but he passed me on to an urologist because he suspected there could be complications. What I imagined was a pretty straightforward examination turned into something far worse. Testicular cancer was diagnosed.

The two surgeons agreed that as the hernia and the cancer were in the same area of my groin both minor procedures could be done under the same anaesthetic. The operation went according to plan and a day later I was back home and making my final preparations to leave on a cruise holiday.

I knew that I was in trouble two days later when I experienced difficulty walking. I returned to the specialist and after a brief check he announced that he would have to operate again that evening.

Septicaemia had set in after the initial operation and that was why the surgeon needed to do the second operation. He really screwed up the second operation and when I regained consciousness I was lying in intensive care with a tangle of pipes sticking out of my throat! For the next five days I hung to life on the thinnest of threads.

Yet again Jeffrey King came to my rescue. He arrived at the hospital, scanned the charts hanging at the foot of the bed and made his own diagnosis. My lungs were flooded and I couldn't get enough oxygen to my heart. Jeffrey took things into his own hands and told the nursing staff to disregard any instructions they'd been given. He prescribed a heavy kind of diuretic tablet that resulted in me losing seven litres of fluid in the following twenty-four hours.

After I returned from my month-long Mediterranean cruise I felt refreshed and my batteries recharged. I went to see Joe Skowno again for my six-month check-up.

"Joe, could it be at all possible for a hernia to re-occur so soon after my operation?"

He looked up and replied, "There's absolutely no chance of that. Why?"

I said, "Well, it's there again."

I dropped my pants and he examined the tender spot. He appeared mystified until he checked his notes. The surgeon had operated on the wrong side! I went back for what I hoped would be the last time but I wasn't brave enough to trust the original surgeon. The operation went off without a hitch and I was on my feet a day later.

Simeka

Chapter 38

Retirement that didn't happen

By 1997 it was time for me to think about retiring from Adcorp. My health was deteriorating and I owed it to myself to begin enjoying the fruits of my business success. I knew that I should consider stepping down.

They say that a major contributor to heart attacks is stress. In my case I have never let it get the better of me. I always perform at the top of my game when I am under pressure and I thrive on the cut and thrust of deal-making.

From the day I walked into the shambles at Admark I had worked toward building a viable business. It was rewarding to think that I had taken a tiny company and turned it into a group that had a turnover of a billion rand a year but as any boxing commentator will tell you—you shouldn't take one fight too many! Many founders of successful businesses commit the cardinal mistake of hanging on too long. I was determined not to let it happen to me. I needed to begin the search for my successor.

When you have been the chief executive for any length of time it is important to take stock of your own performance. As you grow older and hopefully wiser you become more conservative, which is unfortunately a fact of life. You see risk more clearly than you see opportunity. As a younger person starting out on the road you are dynamic, you are bold and you think big but as you mature you drop your sights and the lateral thinking that helped you develop the business in the first place becomes narrower. It is impossible to maintain the same level of energy that one has in the early stages of building a business. I concluded that I should plan for an orderly handover.

After giving my succession plan considerable thought I convened a meeting with all the members of the executive and explained my intentions.

It was absolutely essential to plan my departure in a way that wouldn't be disruptive. There were two aspects to consider. Firstly, I was anxious to convey the right message to all our loyal employees. Secondly, the financial community needed assurance that my exit was planned and that a succession plan would be smoothly executed. At all costs I had to ensure that the Adcorp share price would not be negatively affected.

I advised the executive that once a successor had been chosen I would sell my shares. My entire wealth was tied up in Adcorp and I have never owned a share in any other business. My personal financial advisors often warned me against having all my eggs in one basket and I understood that they had my best interests at heart. However, I had supreme faith in my investment because there was no company I knew better than Adcorp. I understood the company from top to bottom and I had great confidence in its ability to blossom. There was no wavering on this issue. Before I retired I would divest myself of all my equity.

I asked if any member of the executive had aspirations to succeed me. I invited anyone that wished to be considered for the post to meet me privately but I made it clear that if we were unable to make a suitable internal appointment we would begin looking outside the group. I received just one application from an executive member but after a frank and open discussion we agreed that he didn't meet all the criteria.

Each member of our management team was asked to consider carefully what qualities they believed a successor should possess. From their response I was able to summarize the seven key assets that an ideal CEO would need. I compiled a list in order of priority and appointed an executive search specialist to find suitable candidates. I was presented with a short list of five possibilities that I swiftly narrowed down to two. I then dropped a bombshell. I announced that I was taking a back seat when it came to the final choice!

My decision was based on what I believed was sound logic because whoever was appointed as the new CEO wouldn't be answering to me. I felt very strongly that the evaluation process should be conducted by the executive team and that they should select a successor with whom they felt most comfortable.

The final choice was, in boxing terminology, decided on a split decision. The executive voted by four to three. It was a close call and there was a danger that it could result in friction amongst the executive. The die was cast.

Henri Staal was the man chosen to lead Adcorp. He was just thirty-eight but he had a sound track record and prior to his appointment he was the senior consulting partner of Ernst & Young. He had a string of qualifications—a BSc, MSc, MBA, and a doctorate in business, and possessed a rare intellect. In his previous position he was known for his excellent interpersonal skills. In addition, he was very charming and articulate and made a great impression on all of us.

Henri took up his post as CEO and I agreed to work alongside him for nine months. I planned to gradually fade into the background as Henri gained experience and confidence. I made it clear that I was available to consult with him but he would increasingly take responsibility for running the business. I moved to dispel any notion that our employees and the financial community may have harboured that I was making the decisions and not Henri.

Around this time, unbeknown to me, I was entered in the 1998 Entrepreneur of the Year Awards. I was invited to a splendid function for the five finalists and leaders of the business community. The CEO of Discovery, Adrian Gore won the coveted award. Later the judges told me that although there was no official recognition, I had been voted runner-up.

My planned departure from Adcorp, however, was delayed by six months after Henri Staal and the chairman Frederick van Zyl Slabbert approached me to stay on. There were nervous times on the JSE and the entire market had retreated. While Adcorp was unlikely to suffer as badly as some other companies, they were concerned about how the market would react to the timing of my departure. Even though the financial gurus and investors had known of my plans for a while I agreed to remain until mid-2000.

Once again when it was time to go, pressure was applied for me to extend my term of office by yet another six-month period. This time, in spite of the continued bad performance of the JSE, I was decidedly reluctant.

It was my contention that there were no grey areas when I announced my plans to retire. I had made all the right moves to ensure that the financial community was clear about my intentions. A successor had been appointed and he had been met with approval whenever I introduced him to our major investors.

As the saying goes 'a puppy is not just for Christmas' one cannot discard it when it becomes an inconvenience and that's how I viewed my lingering departure. Yet again I was forced to sacrifice my personal plans for the sake of the company. I agreed to stay on but this time I wrote a letter to the board confirming that there would be no extension beyond December 2000.

Toward the end of 2000 I was aware that a rift was developing between Henri Staal and Simeka Management Consulting. It troubled me because Simeka brought Adcorp huge credibility in influential circles and they represented a crucial part of the group's broader empowerment philosophy. When I left for my overseas holiday in August I believed that the rumblings were no more than a minor locking of horns. I had no idea that it was the prelude to the dissolution of the partnership between the two companies.

In the space of just twenty-one days the festering dispute had turned into open conflict. In my absence Simeka had arranged a management buyout from Adcorp. Agreement had been reached between the two parties and legal documents had been drawn up. Seemingly there was no chance to reverse the dispute that had led to the fragmentation of the relationship.

Simeka was a key strategic element within Adcorp. Because of its visibility and high-quality operational management, in my opinion, the decision to split was a blunder of epic proportions. It was a travesty that a fully empowered growth partner was allowed to leave under such circumstances.

I left Adcorp at the end of 2000 and was honoured at a wonderful farewell dinner at the Atrium. To my delight I was granted my special request. Buskaids, a wonderful classically trained string orchestra from

Soweto was invited to play for us. Many old faces were at the dinner including all three of my personal assistants and it was both a sad and exciting occasion. From time to time employees that I've known for years cross my path and I am always happy to see them. Although I am no longer at Adcorp it will always have an important place in my heart.

Chapter 39

A new era and a new challenge

I needed to ascertain whether Simeka's differences with Adcorp were irreconcilable as I still held out hope that I could change their minds. They stood firm and to a man they confirmed that there was no possibility that they would return to the Adcorp fold. My relationship with Simeka Management Consulting had always been on a very firm footing and therefore I wasn't surprised when they approached me to assist them with their management buyout.

I informed Adcorp management of Simeka's approach and they indicated that they had no objection to my involvement.

On January 1st 2001 I moved seamlessly into my new position at Simeka. My planned retirement stretched to a public holiday and a New Year's Eve party! The sale of my Adcorp shares had left me free of financial worries. It was passion and not money that attracted me to Simeka. I was driven by my desire to encourage a talented, ambitious, professional group of people to realize their goal.

I was thrilled to be part of an exiting empowerment company and we consummated the deal. Once the funding was in place, the management and shareholders at Simeka invited me to join them in their fledgling independent venture.

I was delighted to be reunited with Sheila Snelling who at one time was my PA at Adcorp. We had remained in touch ever since she had moved to Simeka and it had been satisfying for me to watch her steady progress. Her PA days were behind her; she had begun to realize her full potential and had spread her wings to become a fully fledged member of the management team.

In return for putting up the finance for the buyout I acquired a 50% stake in Simeka Investment Holdings. Our vision was to work toward creating wealth for the shareholders and eventually to achieve a JSE listing. I agreed that should I elect to leave Simeka or sell my shares that they would receive preference at a favourable PE rating. I had immense faith in the ability of the Simeka management team but they were still young and lacked commercial experience. We decided that I would offer guidance in helping them to determine a vision and a strategy.

There is no other reason to start a business unless you genuinely believe that you can create wealth. That is the only thing that makes the headaches and heartaches of owning a business worthwhile. My advice for people when they are contemplating going into business for themselves is that it is better to work for an employer if the sole reason for starting up is to earn a good salary.

If one sets out to create wealth one must bear in mind that above all else it is essential to create something that somebody else one day will believe is worth buying. I urged Simeka Investment Holdings to pursue the same objectives that had brought success to Adcorp. Together we devised a vision and a strategy:

- Never enter any business you don't clearly understand.
- Only employ the very best staff.
- Remain in arenas of strong growth.
- Ensure that the price of your service is not your sole measure.
- Recognize that somebody else will always offer a cheaper option.
- Strive to be the #1 in all operational areas.
- Be confident to charge premium rates.
- Diversify within areas of expertise, but only when established.

In following the same ideals it would be easy to suggest that Simeka simply became a clone of Adcorp. This is simply untrue because we operated in completely different service arenas. Simeka has become a shooting star—a company destined to join the big league one day.

In 2001 when Simeka secured a tender in excess of quarter of a million rands (almost all business was won through the tender process) we threw a party. By mid-2004 it was commonplace for Simeka to win tenders of between ten and twenty million rands.

Simeka's clear vision allied to its credibility and delivery capability has turned a small company with a big vision into a success story. It is a matter of some sadness for me that Adcorp let such a superb business slip through its fingers.

Our primary objective was to attain a JSE listing within five years (or at any time that it deemed to be opportune) but in the longer term Simeka set their sights on generating an annual after tax-profit of twenty million rands. In 2004 they were already well on the road to achieving their aim.

By 2001 the lion's share of management consulting contracts were being put out to tender by the government and by parastatals. Empowerment was a key issue in almost all tender documents and as a result it was highly unlikely that any company without a genuine commitment to it would have been successful in gaining any tender.

This requirement created a unique situation and led to considerable frustration for Simeka. The 'big five' audit and management consulting practices were essentially white-owned and they were locked into cross-shareholding agreements with their international parent companies. Few of them possessed even superficial equity empowerment credentials. To allow these traditional companies to enter any tender process they needed an empowerment partner. They often turned to Simeka for the answer.

The traditional 'big five' consulting practices were the only entities capable of handling large-sized projects and they invited Simeka to join them in various ad hoc joint ventures. These were early days in Simeka's development and they welcomed the chance to become involved because they needed the work. The downside was that after the tender was secured and the cake was divided Simeka was left to scramble for the crumbs. The big five continued to call the shots because at that stage Simeka lacked the muscle power to compete at the implementation level.

I decided to accompany Simeka's MD, Barry Fraser, to discuss the ethics of these once-off partnerships with the management of one of the big five constituencies. I needed to challenge them over their attitude toward Simeka as it struck me that they viewed us as dispensable—to be cast off once the tender came to an end.

I wanted to explain to them at the meeting that this endless cycle of marriage and divorce had no empowerment benefit whatsoever and that furthermore it flew against the spirit of government policy. By using Simeka as a convenience there was absolutely no skills transfer and no attempt was being made to broaden their experience. This short-sighted policy saw Simeka living from project to project, powerless to implement any kind of forward planning strategy. When it was my turn to speak I was very voluble, "Surely you realize that this policy of calling us in only when it suits you is not genuine empowerment. Try to look ahead, times are changing. Explain to me the sense in drifting from one short-term empowerment relationship to another. There's no continuity in that policy. You need to nurture and develop a relationship with one partner. If you persist in taking a series of girlfriends you will end up on the shelf. In short you need to get a wife."

My argument fell on deaf ears and we returned to our office fiercely determined that even if it meant that we would grow more slowly we would row our own boat. It took courage for Barry to advise the big-brother partners that we were no longer interested in joining them in any future tender. We cut ourselves adrift but in doing so we became masters of our own destiny. We didn't want to grovel for crumbs again.

That decision had a delightfully ironic twist. By 2004 Simeka were winning huge projects against all comers and sometimes the projects were so large that we were forced to outsource some of the work to the big five!

There is no doubt that the big five still command a massive slice of the market but if they had possessed just a smidgen of foresight they would have accepted our offer of long-term empowerment partnership. If they had taken this bold step they would have found themselves in an unassailable position today. Fortune does indeed favour the brave.

The timid approach by those companies to empowerment left the door open for Simeka to grow dramatically. Who could have imagined that one day very senior members of the big five would begin to defect to Simeka! The big five management consultancies are owned by auditing firms and none of the consulting employees are genuine stakeholders. Once they join Simeka they are given the opportunity to own equity and thus take the first tottering steps toward creating personal wealth rather than working for a salary package. This new breed of consultant has the foresight to realize that the old traditional consultancies do not have a hope of competing with Simeka once it grows to a significant size, when empowerment is one of the tender criteria. I am confident that in the very near future the 'big five' will be joined by Simeka in a new look 'big six'.

Simeka Management Consulting was founded by two dynamic young twenty-eight-year-olds, Barry Fraser and Robinson Ramaite. I was first attracted by their moral and ethical approach to business and after seven years their burning passion has not diminished.

Barry, the CEO, and I have a very special relationship and I often refer to him as my third son. We lost the services of Robinson for three years when he was asked to join government to serve as Director-General of the Public Service, but he later rejoined the company.

Barry's sister is Geraldine Fraser Moleketi and his brother-in-law is Jabu Moleketi who was appointed Deputy Minister of Finance in 2004. Both Barry and Robinson come from a politically aware background and they were part of the youth movement swept up in the tragedy of apartheid. However, since becoming integrated into business neither has sought to use their political clout to secure contracts. I have never heard either of them express any personal grievances over the injustices of the past. Simeka pitch for work based solely on the most powerful of weapons—ability and integrity.

It became an important part of our philosophy in growing Simeka that we would never further our objectives by giving in to tempting but meaningless business opportunities. On many occasions Simeka executives were approached by companies that needed an empowerment partner to help win a contract. Although it would have been a fast-track to wealth they refused these overtures unless their skills and abilities were required. They rejected offers where all that was being sought was their empowerment credentials.

I had already achieved a measure of personal success and so I did not attempt to influence their decisions but to their enormous credit they never entertained a thought about pursuing a dead-end partnership. We steadfastly adhered to our principles of staying on the double highway. We had set ourselves that vision and to veer off course would be a betrayal.

In the past our growth was often inhibited because we chose to take the moral high ground and after seven years there is no doubt that our principles have been fully vindicated. Simeka refuse to be drawn into partnership with any organization that wants nothing more than the ability to 'colour-up' their tender proposal. Often these companies have invited Simeka to take 25% equity in a joint venture, but recoil at the thought of actually allowing them to become involved in the project. These proposals are not only immoral but they debase the government empowerment objectives. Unless we can add real value to any partnership and we can keep our hand firmly on the tiller, we will continue to shy away.

In mid-2004 a major financial institution showed great interest in Simeka. Not only did they see the worth of the company but they saw the added value that lay in its ability to drive them forward into suitable acquisitions. This course of action would significantly enhance the size of field of operation of Simeka. The empowerment shareholding in Simeka was of course one of their obvious key areas of interest.

It followed that after this approach it no longer suited the company to have me on board as a shareholder. I very clearly understood their position as I had always recognized the importance of the empowerment shareholding within Simeka.

I respected their stance and readily acceded to their request as I believed that the primary reason of my involvement with them had been achieved. They had blossomed into a company of consequence and well worthy of consideration by a significant outside party.

After a short negotiation, I agreed to sell my 50% shareholding for five million rands. This transaction was finally completed in December 2004 and it was with a degree of pleasure that I noted that in May of 2005 Simeka sold 100% of the company for forty-eight million rands.

My belief in their ability had been vindicated by the worthwhile commitment that they had made and the single-minded path they had followed that ultimately led to their success.

Since my departure from Simeka at the end of 2004 I have founded a new company, Khululeka Corporate Services (Pty) Ltd. The sole objective will be to match companies that seek empowerment partners, with appropriate suitors. Khululeka is staffed with a number of my long-term empowerment partners with whom I was associated during my days at Adcorp. We are the exclusive associates of First National Bank in finding empowerment partners. They have a large portfolio of clients who recognize the need and importance of changing the empowerment face of their various companies.

As business moves forward there is no doubt that any company of any size will founder on the rocks if they fail to heed the message of empowerment. I know that once again the opportunity that lies ahead has limitless horizons.

Life

Chapter 40

Humanizing passions

My father inhabited a world where men kept a stiff upper lip and little boys didn't cry. His Victorian attitudes meant that he kept his distance and he set greater store by discipline rather than love and affection. Men never expressed emotion and they barely hugged their wives let alone their children.

My strict upbringing and my years at boarding school have rubbed off and many of my father's traits have been ingrained in me. I am not proud of it and I know that I wasn't a particularly good father. Even though my children were the centre of my universe and I loved them to bits, I just had problems showing affection. In their formative years they suffered and I am sorry. Delia was just two and Sean was three and a half when I was divorced. Circumstances dictated that I was given custody of them but my constant trips away and busy working life deprived them of what they needed most—a father that showed them unconditional love. Their childhood was disruptive and unbalanced and it was hardly surprising that our relationship became severely strained. I am eternally grateful that time does indeed heal all wounds and now that they are adults, I know they have forgiven me.

My relationship with my children is radically different nowadays and maybe we are stronger for what we have been through. We now share wonderful times together and I am at my very happiest when we are just sitting around and behaving like a proper loving family, usually talking about the bush and beloved Ingwelala. My friends and family are the cornerstones of my life. They add to its quality and enrich it and I have to stop and remind myself never to take them for granted.

After five years of a pretty miserable home existence Wendi came into my life and it was the most fantastic thing that has ever happened to me. Within six months of meeting we were married and had moved into our home in Craighall with our four children (two of hers and two of mine). At long last all six of us could begin to share a stable, loving family life. Sadly, Wendi's youngest son drowned in a tragic accident soon after we were married but her other son, Myles—now bigger and better looking than me—are very close.

Wendi is a very special person and anybody that ever has contact with her will say the same. Nobody can fail to be touched by her kind and thoughtful nature, and her generosity knows no bounds. However frustrated or annoyed she may become I have yet to hear her utter a bad word about anyone. She is the kind of person that tackles any task with gusto, she grabs life by the throat and squeezes every last drop from it. She has an almost childlike love of nature and is passionate about wildlife and her painting.

Wendi possess another gift that I would do anything to have! We both love golf but whereas I tend to brood after a bad round she has the capacity to forget the poor shots when she shoots over a hundred. She will never make reference to a hook or a muffed putt and it is sufficient for her to derive pleasure from the perfect drives and chips in her round. She is everything to me and she is at the heart of any plans or thinking that I ever indulge in.

Wendi never questions my business decisions but always lends her full support to anything that I attempt. It must have been hard for her at times but somehow she always managed to understand that I needed to do things my way.

I count myself extremely fortunate to own a house and a share in

Ingwelala Game Reserve. Ingwelala is a quite spectacular tract of virgin bush right inside the Kruger National Park and is blessed with more than its fair share of lions and elephants. I never tire of the bush and every time that I visit I manage to see something new and exciting.

During my years at Adcorp I used to rush away from the office late on Friday afternoon for the six-and-a-half-hour drive. Then we would have to pack up and return after lunch on Sundays. There is a landing strip in the reserve and nowdays we usually take a short flight from Lanseria and turn our stays into real long weekends. We visit Ingwelala six times a year, usually with friends that share our love of the bush and it gives me immense pleasure to be able to host them for a few days. Our children too visit the reserve with their friends and they have inherited my love of the wild. I find nothing more rewarding than to spend a day game-viewing and then to wind down with sundowners and a braai round the campfire. Only in South Africa are we so privileged to experience the bush in this way.

Some friends jokingly say that I am obsessed by elephants but that is hardly fair! Perhaps they base their observation on the fact that the walls of my office and bar at home are covered with photos of jumbos! They are, I will concede, my favourites but if I had to list the runner-up it would certainly be the hyena.

That may seem like a strange choice—I certainly don't think that hyenas would appear in most peoples' top ten, but perhaps I should explain.

A family of hyenas has been part of our Ingwelala household for fifteen years. It all began when a hyena research project was being conducted. Rangers fitted four females with different-coloured tracking collars. The idea behind the project was to ascertain how far the hyenas' territory extended and how often they visited various parts of it. The hyena with the yellow collar seemed to take an instant liking to our stoep. I didn't know how far she went during the day but whenever we were visiting she would arrive as darkness descended. This went on for quite a while until about a year later she appeared with a cub in tow. The cub looked as if it was about four months old.

Six weeks later on our next visit the cub appeared on cue but there was no sign of its mother. It was another two years before yellow collar showed up again and she crept on to the stoep and quietly lay down. We threw her a couple of bones which she crunched up noisily before wandering off. Yellow collar visited us regularly over the next three years and during that time she bought three new additions to her family to show us.

We began to recognize the hyenas by their markings and we gave them all names. The eldest of yellow collar's offspring must be about ten or eleven by now and about two years ago she bought her own cub to our stoep.

Whenever we visit Ingwelala I can hardly wait for darkness to fall. Unfailingly on our first evening as many as three hyenas arrive and park themselves on the stoep right outside the door of our cottage. They wait patiently for our braai to end and they know that at the end of it I will collect up all the bones for them. I find hyenas highly intelligent animals and they look me in the eye in much the same way as a dog would. They almost seem to know when it is the right time for them to go. If ever they become intrusive all I have to do is clap or raise my finger and they discreetly disappear into the night.

Apart from the time when we found a pair of leopards lying on our stoep our most spectacular moment at Ingwelala was the evening when we stumbled across the carcass of a fully grown male giraffe. We were out in the Land Rover at dusk when we spotted the fallen giraffe with three lionesses and three cubs feeding from the kill. One of the lionesses was the last known white lion in the wild. It was a magical moment. Of all the photos that I've taken at Ingwelala, my shot of the lioness and her cubs feeding on the rump of the giraffe, takes pride of place.

We returned to the carcass every morning and afternoon over the next two days but soon two of the lionesses moved on. The white lion was left alone with her three cubs which, unlike their mother, were a natural colour. After a couple of days the giraffe was stiff with rigor mortis and the cubs were using the giraffe's neck to slide from the horns to the shoulder! Sadly, two years after that first unforgettable sighting, the white lion was attacked and killed by a rival pride.

The television and print media have recently given significant coverage to the two white lion cubs, born on our reserve. Their birth was filmed by an Ingwelela owner.

Nowadays I enjoy travelling purely for pleasure with Wendi at my side. Happily my days of toting a briefcase to meetings all over the globe, often arriving late at night and then having to check into a faceless hotel are behind me. Now I go anywhere exotic where there are blue skies and golden beaches—cities aren't really for me. In the last few years we have enjoyed our annual cruise, sometimes in the Far East but often in the Mediterranean.

I can best describe my on-and-off romance with golf as a frustration rather than a passion. Sometimes I think that there must be some deep-seated psychological reason for this self-imposed torture! There is nothing in my life that I have tried so hard to master and yet have met with such singular lack of success! A bad round can drive me to distraction and on more than one occasion I have threatened to give my clubs away. My friends joke at my expense because they know that the feeling will quickly wear off and that it won't be long before I am ready to indulge in the next round of masochism!

One time at Glendower I actually drove four successive balls off the tee and into the water. Instead of breaking the driver over my knee, I sent it and my three wood flying into the dam after the balls! Even after this ignominious display of petulance I was still determined to play the shot. Unfortunately when I looked in my bag there were only irons and putters left! I walked across to the ladies tee, helped myself to a wood from Wendi's bag, teed up and drove number five straight into the water followed by her driver! It cost me a new set of woods.

Twice a year we drive down to our other home in Selborne Golf Estate on the Natal South Coast. Selborne has often been described as South Africa's prettiest course and our house overlooks the sixteenth hole. At dusk, bushbuck come down to drink at the water that surrounds our veranda, I love the quiet and calm atmosphere there.

The estate was the brainchild and dream of Denis Barker, a wealthy dairy farmer. He had a vision to turn a tract of virgin bush into an exclusive quality estate. He enjoyed the luxury of not having to build it with the intention of creating profit. He called in Ola Grinaker to help and together with great imagination and a liberal splash of inspiration they fulfilled and far surpassed their wildest dreams.

I thought that I'd finally cracked the answer to my golfing problems in 2003. I went to see Muss Gammon, the well-known teaching professional and he helped me to iron out a few technical faults. I couldn't wait for the opportunity to get out on to the course. It went without saying that my friends shared my new-found optimism.

I was elated with my first few rounds when I got my score for nine holes down from the 50s to 41 and I was convinced that I was now on my way. As the holiday progressed my score crept up and up until I couldn't break 50 again. It was a bitter disappointment and after another shocking round one of the caddies was again very close to inheriting a free set of clubs!

Personal crusades

Chapter 41

Stamping out corruption

Good corporate governance is very close to my heart and I am zealous in my pursuit of it. I conduct workshops and speak about its importance to audiences throughout the country. In my discussions with businessmen across the board I am surprised to find that government-controlled parastatals appear to take good corporate governance more seriously than many listed companies. It never ceases to amaze me how often high-profile individuals, some with the morals of an alley cat, are able to single-handedly sink major corporations.

South African public companies are primarily regulated by the rules of the Johannesburg Stock Exchange and by the King Report. In earlier times the first report known as King 1 contained sufficient legislation and guidance to close every conceivable loophole in corporate law. Over time unscrupulous businessmen have managed to find ways to circumvent many of the rules. Human nature dictates that some individuals will find ways to exploit rules and they will not hesitate to resort to creative crookery. The injustice of it all is that so many escape unscathed.

In my opinion South Africa needs to take a close look at business and take time out to reassess what has gone wrong. Corruption is rife and while I may be accused of being an idealist I believe that it cannot be stamped out until our morals and ethics change.

Mandela, Ghandi and Mother Theresa symbolize everything that is pure. To achieve greatness and change much of the world they didn't find it necessary to worm around the rule book. It sickens me to the pit of my stomach when I compare these icons with the greedy, grasping and corrupt men who have contributed to the demise of organizations such as Enron and Parmelat. In the pursuit of personal enrichment the executives of these companies took shelter behind a bunch of corrupt auditors and merchant bankers. They stand guilty of encouraging these so-called professionals to plumb the moral depths.

I spent a lifetime building a business and along the way I accumulated knowledge. I now spend much time on platforms where I address boards and senior management on how, and more importantly, how not to conduct corporate governance. I will take whatever remedial action I can to help eradicate the scourge of corporate malpractice. I have launched my crusade by suggesting a few fundamental and practical steps that I firmly believe will go a long way toward curing the malaise. Almost every major corporate collapse has been bought about by the misdeeds of just one or two top executives. I do not subscribe to the notion that the introduction of more curbs or regulatory measures will curtail corporate malpractice. An ever expanding set of rules didn't help in the USA and it won't solve South Africa's problems either.

South Africa needs a complete change of mindset to put the brake on runaway corruption. Corrupt practice can only exist within a large public company if there are greedy and unethical top executives surrounded by non-executive directors lacking in knowledge who are willing to engage inept and compliant auditors and then encourage them to close their eyes to their dirty work.

In my opinion any auditor found guilty of signing off false financial reports should have their professional qualifications cancelled. I would make it illegal for them to ever practise in South Africa again. Furthermore I would name and shame them in every national newspaper. Just a handful of cases would be enough to frighten off any auditor tempted to engage in fraudulent accounting practices.

As I look around I am disheartened to note a new and disturbing trend. Listed companies are beginning to increase the number of non-executive directors on their boards as if it will provide some kind of overnight solution. Their thinking is flawed and it does not get to the root of the problem.

Non-executive directors are expected to be people of honour and integrity and their function is to counterbalance any possible excesses of the executive directors. This is all very laudable, but what is abundantly clear is that most of them lack a vital ingredient. Few have even a rudimentary knowledge of the inner workings of the company that appoints them. The mere act of increasing the number of non-executive directors on a board doesn't necessarily add value. Executive directors will always be able to give non-executive directors the run-around because they have more knowledge. Knowledge is power and because of it executive directors will always be able to manipulate and outwit the non-executive board members.

It serves no purpose when a non-executive attends a board meeting, keeps quiet, contributes nothing and collects a fat fee on the way out. The answer is education.

The JSE should make it mandatory for non-executive directors to spend two or three days a month at the company on whose board they sit. Pay them for their services by all means, but ensure that they spend quality time with the managing director, financial director, sales and marketing director or whoever else can assist them to understand what is going on. Perhaps then they will be able to make informed decisions at board meetings.

Chapter 42

Spreading the word

Lecturing is something else that I enjoy immensely now that I have a little more spare time. I find it both stimulating and satisfying to be able to share some of the knowledge that I have gained during my years in business. Although I still think of myself first and foremost as a marketing man I have also accumulated experience in mergers and acquisitions. Because of my track record at both Adcorp and Simeka I am frequently called upon to talk on the subject.

The first time I lectured was when I agreed to address an audience at Wits MBA Graduate School. It was shortly after Adcorp won the Top 100 JSE Companies Award so my star was in the ascendancy. The students were almost finished a sponsored intensive six-week course, by one of the big five audit companies, on mergers and acquisitions. I was scheduled to be the final speaker.

Before I agreed to speak I asked for the course notes so that I wouldn't bore the audience by covering old ground. I wanted to amplify what had already been said and weave my talk into what had already been taught.

I noted that the students had been bombarded with details of finance, accounting and administration. They had explored assets and liabilities, agreements, licences, royalties, rebates, discounts and every conceivable aspect of due diligence and auditing. The course was comprehensive but I was surprised to find that none of the other lecturers had remotely touched on the most important issue. Nothing had been said about people!

I was introduced to the audience of about sixty MBAs and was given a brief resumé of my business credentials. I stood at the podium, surveyed the audience and opened my talk with a question, "Can somebody tell me what they think is the most valuable asset in any company?"

A young lady raised her hand and replied, "I think the staff is a company's greatest asset."

There was a general murmur of agreement among the audience.

"We are in agreement so far. Will anyone venture to voice an opinion about who they think are the most important of all those employees? Not only that, I would like someone to explain why that is the case."

A hand shot up from a man near the back of the auditorium, "I think that it is the company management. They are the people that give direction, develop strategy, provide leadership and create a culture and a philosophy."

I was struck by how well he had articulated his thoughts.

"Thank you. I agree with you totally. But can I tell you what puzzles me? You have all spent an exhausting six weeks delving into every corner of mergers and acquisitions. You all seem to agree that people and management top the list of assets yet you haven't spent a moment discussing the subject!"

The audience began to shuffle in their seats. I could see that they had become noticeably more attentive. I could sense that they were warming to my argument.

"I have very strong views as you can probably detect. Many companies are headed by financial people. Often their bid to acquire a company is driven purely by financial considerations. I sometimes despair when I listen to interviews and read articles in which they rationalize their latest acquisition. They say—we are going to add one and one and get two and a quarter—but in reality that rarely happens."

I caught the eye of one of the audit comapny executives and he appeared discomfited by my line of reasoning, but I continued, "Let me tell you what usually occurs. When they find out that one plus one only makes two, they immediately merge the companies in the hope of enhancing profits. They cut costs by slashing staff. What they should be doing is growing both businesses independently. Only then will one and one equal two and a quarter. In that way they will increase their profits and they will create new jobs in the process."

There was a general nod of approval and my logic seemed to be making sense to them. "Perhaps I am biased but this is because my businesses all depended on the performance of my people. I never embarked on the acquisition trail with the intention of squeezing out extra profits from the company I'd bought by cutting costs. My philosophy was only to buy businesses that had intrinsic value. I viewed the worth of any organization I wanted to acquire by examining the value of the people that created the business and the people that managed it. I think that it is crucial to keep those people on board after any acquisition. Then by adding value to those businesses perhaps you can truly make one plus one equal two and a quarter."

My lecture happened to coincide with the hostile bid for Standard Bank by Nedbank. As it happened it didn't materialize but at the time it threatened to be the biggest acquisition in South African history. I asked the audience, "What do you think will happen if Nedbank is successful? Let me answer my own question. If past experience is anything to go by, the Standard Bank management will feel vulnerable. Most of them will opt for the golden parachutes that Nedbank will be dangling in front of their noses. Nedbank will think that they have made huge savings but in doing so they will have lost the very people that made Standard Bank attractive in the first place. Undoubtedly Nedbank will underrate the value of corporate culture at Standard Bank as well. This culture permeates through any organization and an alien culture cannot be imposed on another company overnight whether it is Nedbank or anyone else. It just doesn't work."

I wrapped up my talk by urging the audience to think again and to think about people and not just the financial angle when entering into a potential acquisition negotiation.

My speech stirred more passion and was more thought-provoking than any of their due diligence lectures. It was contentious and not at all what they had had in mind, so I wasn't unduly worried or surprised that I wasn't invited back.

Epilogue

Chapter 43

Lessons learned

My dictionary defines happiness as —joy, exhilaration, bliss, contentedness delight, enjoyment and satisfaction. It tells me that it is 'a peaceful kind of content in which one rests without desires even though every wish may not have been granted'.

Reduced to a string of words its attainment seems pretty easy but it begs a few questions.

Why isn't everybody happy? Why are there so many unhappy people? Is it important to be happy?

Most folk I know have to work hard at being happy. To attain happiness they must follow very different paths. Introspection may produce many of the answers. It is self-knowledge that enables one to see clearly and it provides a roadmap. However, in the end you learn that the journey is more important than the destination.

I constantly remind myself and my children how important it is to strive for happiness. Not everybody can achieve happiness in the same way and it doesn't come without conditions. It is a state that shouldn't be gained at the expense of another person although occasionally, inadvertently, somebody may be hurt along the way. You must come to terms with what you hold important in life even though your aspirations may change as you mature and grow.

You must tackle the cause of your unhappiness and strive to change it. You shouldn't continue to live in an unhappy relationship or persist with a job if it makes you unhappy. Do whatever it takes to improve the situation but when nothing more can be done put it behind you and move on.

Many people judge success purely in terms of wealth and they believe that if only they were rich they would be happy. Of course money is important because day-to-day living is a constant struggle, but one only has to look at the shattered personal lives of so many rich and famous people to realize that money does not guarantee happiness.

I always ask myself "Is it reasonable?" It's amazing how often we do the wrong things and take the wrong decisions because we follow others. If only we asked ourselves "Is it reasonable?" we would have often taken a better path. I believe that it is preferable to do the wrong thing for the right reason than the right thing for all the wrong reasons. Perhaps one may be tempted to do otherwise in times of stress or out of adversity or even to gain a short-term benefit. In doing the wrong thing for the right reasons you can usually learn a valuable lesson. The next time the same situation arises, you will probably be able to make the right decision for the right reason.

In business, the quality that I prize above all others is vision, but it is essential not to drop your guard. One must constantly re-focus as one moves forward. From clear vision springs the need to communicate that vision to everyone involved. Unless you can persuade the people that surround you to buy into your philosophies you cannot reasonably expect them to implement them. Time and time again I have emphasized how vital it is that the person leading a company should care passionately about excellence. This is not only applicable to their own performance but it extends to their ability to communicate it to their staff, customers and suppliers.

As I became wise in the ways of company acquisitions I learned that many of the people I was dealing with were far less experienced in this field than I was. I was a veteran of many acquisition deals and often

I faced people who were going through the process for the first time. It would have been easy to take advantage of their inexperience and secure a better financial deal for the company. Fortunately, I learned very early on that in doing a clever deal I would have lost their respect. It wouldn't have taken long for them to realize that they had been duped and within no time they would have become disenchanted and their passion would dissipate.

While management creates vision, philosophy and strategy, it cannot drive the company forward without staff of the very highest calibre. Those staff must not only be cherished but management must constantly seek to demonstrate and underscore their value.

Invariably owners of business glibly tell me that their customer is the focus of their business. Too often, 'The customer is always right' are mere words. Action speaks volumes and if you believe fervently that your business relies on your customers the credo must be enforced and understood at all levels. Many businessmen fail to recognize how vitally important suppliers are to the success of their organization. I think back to my early days at Admark and realize that if our creditors hadn't agreed to keep us afloat, life may have been very different for me.

The ability to identify talented people early in their careers can never be underrated. These rough diamonds should be nurtured and encouraged to become shining stars. I have heard businessmen complain that they have developed individuals and helped them to achieve their potential only to have them defect to the opposition camp. This obvious risk should never become a deterrent because in the long run the benefits always outweigh any disadvantages. To optimize one's own strength one must optimize the strengths of every single individual in the organization.

In drawing my narrative to a close I would dearly love to gaze into my crystal ball and predict the way that business will be done in twenty years' time. But that would be missing the point—I am not a futurist and I do not have the capability to sketch scenarios. I don't even embrace the latest technology comfortably. No, I will continue to do what I do best and that is to identify opportunities and then direct my energies into turning my vision into business success.

I believe passionately in transformation and empowerment and my mission is to seek to enhance these critical areas in our society.

Appendix

Adcorp awards won

Recruitment advertising

For twelve years Adcorp companies scooped an average that was never less than 50% of the awards at the annual *Sunday Times* Recruitment Advertising Award ceremony. It was a strong indicator of the excellence of the companies that we had within the group. On three occasions we won 70%.

Personnel agencies
- In a national poll of all companies in all business categories DAV Personnel Agency was voted in 2004 as being the fifth-most desirable company in South Africa to work for.
- In both 2004 and 2005 they received the Diamond Award as the best personnel agency in the country.
- In 2006 DAV won the award for the best company to work for in South Africa.

Market research
South African Market Research Awards:

1982 - JPS award - best paper
1986 - JPS award - best paper

1987 - JPS award - best paper
1989 - MRA plate
1989 - JPS award - best paper
1990 - JPS award - best paper
1990 - AMRO award for standards
1991 - AMRO award for standards
1993 - Impact innovation award
1994 - MRA plate
1995 - Impact Innovation Award
1996 - SAMRA trophy - best paper
1996 - MRA plate
1998 - SAMRA trophy - best paper
1999 - MRA award
2000 - Marketing Researcher of the year
2002 - SAMRA trophy - best paper
2003 - SAMRA trophy - best paper
2004 - SAMRA trophy - best paper

ESOMAR:
1999 – Paris - best paper of the conference

PR and Communications:
Simeka/TWS: Three times winners of 'Best PR & Communications Company' in South Africa
Three times winners of 'Best Large PR communications Company'

Management consulting:
Simeka Management Consultancy: Three years in a row – 'Best Strategic Consultancy to Government'

Group:
Adcorp Winner JSE Top 100 Company in 1999